HOW TO KEEP YOUR
STAFF
PRODUCTIVE AND HAPPY

DENIS L. CAUVIER
DENIS L. CAUVIER SEMINARS

KENDALL/HUNT PUBLISHING COMPANY
4050 Westmark Drive   Dubuque, Iowa   52002

Copyright © 1995 by Denis L. Cauvier Seminars

ISBN 0-7872-0572-9

All rights reserved. No part of this publication may be reproduced, stored in a retrieval system, or transmitted, in any form or by any means, electronic, mechanical, photocopying, recording, or otherwise, without the prior written permission of the copyright owner.

Printed in the United States of America
10 9 8 7 6 5 4 3 2 1

This book is dedicated to:

Sam—my first daughter who dances to the beat of her own drum

Stevie—my second daughter who finds laughter and delight in everything she does

and above all,
Debbie,
you are the consummate manager—
you constantly keep our family productive and happy.

Contents

Acknowledgements   *vii*
Personal Note   *ix*

Chapter One: Pulling Out the Red Carpet   **1**

Chapter Two: Training and Developing Your Key Source . . . Your Staff   **23**

Chapter Three: Motivating Staff: Fact or Fiction   **85**

Chapter Four: Becoming an Exceptional Leader   **107**

Chapter Five: Performance Appraisals   **143**

Chapter Six: Correcting Performance Problems with Positive Discipline   **185**

Appendices

I	**209**
II	**216**
III	**223**
IV	**236**
V	**239**

ACKNOWLEDGEMENTS

You can search the early evening sky a long time and find only one or two stars. After a long wait, another appears, then the next, and then a few more. Those you squint at to keep in sight are finally joined by a myriad of stars that seem to appear all at once.

And so it has been with writing this book. I'm grateful for the many who show their support now, but I am especially appreciative of those few stars who shone through the early stages of this project.

To begin, I must thank my best friend and wife Debbie. She constantly supported me in the writing of this book by allowing me the time and space to think and create.

Secondly, I would like to thank my colleagues and friends for sharing their expertise so generously: Bill Gibson, Diane G. King, Bill Grant, David Rich and Shane Gibson.

Thirdly, I must acknowledge some special people who have had an impact on my life. To Bill Kay and the wonderful team at Kendall/Hunt Publishing, thank you for your patience and support. To Linda at Farr/Spriggs Reporting, Inc., thanks for all the technical support. To my parents Roch and Lillian Cauvier for your continued faith, and to all my colleagues and friends from whom I have had the pleasure of learning.

Lastly, I wish to acknowledge the tens of thousands of people who have attended my seminars. I have learned and grown so much as a direct result of your feedback.

How to Keep Your Staff Productive and Happy, is the product of over twelve years of managing numerous employees in various situations. Although the bulk of the book deals with lessons learned through direct experience, a great deal of what I know today was gleaned from a fairly relentless program of self-education, attending countless seminars and workshops and reading management development books at every given opportunity. This book draws together the best of the ideas I was exposed to over the years. Although I have made considerable effort to indicate the source of any words that are not mine, I may have inadvertently failed to acknowledge the original source. If this has occurred I would be pleased to receive any information regarding the proper identification of sources.

A Personal Note From Denis L. Cauvier

Dear Reader,

This book was written to help business leaders, owners, managers, and executives deal more effectively, right now, with their number one issue — dealing with the "people" side of their businesses. Businesses in North America are experiencing a growing concern for the level of productivity of their employees. Statistics have shown that not only is productivity slowly decreasing, but the available qualified work force is shrinking as well. No longer can employers feel that, when a good employee leaves the company, they'll "easily find someone else just as good." Now, more than ever, employers feel the need to hang on to their current productive employees.

The American Hotel & Motel Association released a study in 1992 showing how various factors influenced productivity.

Factor	% Increase in Producitiviy
1. Monitoring turnover & absenteeism	32
2. Employee involvement & interaction	27
3. Work standards	29
4. Orientation program	31
5. Training	45
6. Continuing education & development	22
7. Performance reviews	35

The average small - to medium-sized business in North America has had very little training or assistance in the area of setting up operating systems and plans, to ensure they are attracting, selecting, keeping, training, re-training and developing their staff. My first book *How To Hire The Right Person* deals specifically with the issues of attracting and selecting personnel. *How To Keep Your Staff Productive And Happy* will focus on the latter four issues.

The developing and perpetuating of a strong human resource culture, reducing staff turnover and improving effectiveness even in the smallest of businesses, is an absolute must in the turbulent 90's and beyond. This book will assist businesses to prosper while many others will suffer marginal results or fold.

An organization that fully utilizes the information and tools contained in this book can expect to:

- improve the level of leadership and management skills
- reduce staff turnover
- increase employee morale
- enjoy higher levels of staff performance
- spend less time "putting out fires" and managing by the "seat of the pants"
- improved teamwork
- a more productive and proactive human resource culture
- improved sales and profits

To the best of my ability, I have covered everything I know about Keeping Your Staff Productive and Happy, in this book. This book is a summary of what I have learned from my personal experience plus the combined experience of many of my colleagues. I urge you to use the experience of others that has resulted from years of trial, error, and setbacks to your advantage.

Keep referring to this book. Once you have the knowledge of the basics, the odds are in your favour. I sincerely hope you will be inspired to use this manual as a constant source of practical information to ensure that you keep your staff productive and happy.

Best wishes,

Denis L. Cauvier

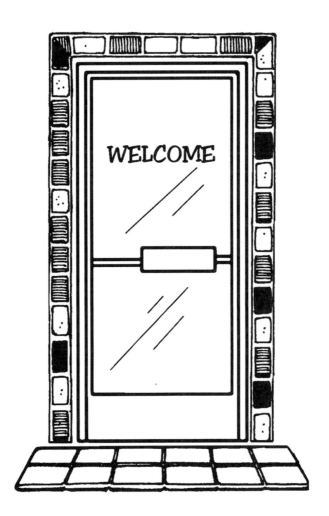

Chapter One

PULLING OUT THE RED CARPET

With the cost of hiring the wrong person at an average of $15,000 per person, it is alarming to learn that approximately one out of every five employees in Canada and the United States will quit or be fired this year. This means that an average 90,000 people will be starting a new job each business day of this year.

One of the primary reasons that people change jobs is that they were never made to feel welcome as a part of the team when they joined. Another big issue is that many people get hired and only have vague notions of what performance is expected of them. As a result, the new employee never really feels connected with the company and his/her original high level of energy soon drops to a level of apathy. Once this occurs, the company will quickly fire the individual to "cut its losses." In other cases the employee, feeling that it is a useless struggle, decides to quit his/her job and try his/her luck elsewhere. Once this happens, the company that he/she just left is once again confronted with the need to find, hire and train someone else.

The role of effective orientation is to assist the new employee to become productive at his/her job as quickly as possible while maintaining the employee's initial level of interest and enthusiasm.

Although orientation costs time and money, to most organizations, these costs are sound investments. Newly-hired employees are seldom capable of fully performing their job duties. Even individuals with experience need to learn about the organization—its people, its policies, and its procedures. They may need training in order to perform successfully. The gap between the new employee's abilities and the job's demands can be substantial.

An employee orientation program can reduce turnover and save an organization thousands of dollars and hundreds of hours of putting out fires.

Whether a company has two employees or 20,000, the orientation of new employees should never be left to chance. Remember, when orientation succeeds, employees succeed. A thorough, well planned, effectively executed orientation is an integral part in keeping your staff productive and happy.

Benefits of Employee Orientation

Helps keep new staff **HAPPY**
- feel at ease and welcomed;
- feel good about company; and
- reinforce employee's decision.

Helps keep new staff **PRODUCTIVE**
- standard of performance;
- teach basics;
- starting point for training and development;
- reduce mistakes and save time; and
- reduce turnover.

Most new employees start off with a great deal of energy, enthusiasm and excitement. They are eager to prove to management that they were a good hiring decision. The atmosphere created during the orientation program can greatly affect what happens to this person's level of interest. A quality orientation will help the employee feel good about his/her new employer. With the new hire feeling at ease and welcomed, his/her decision to join the company will be positively reinforced. In a nutshell, what I am saying is that one of the biggest benefits of orientation is the happiness the staff feels.

The second major benefit incurred by orientation is an increase in productivity. Ken Blanchard, in his book "The One Minute Manager," talks of how he believes in passing out the final exam during the first day of class. Blanchard does this because he wants his students to understand right from day one what performance standards are expected. I support this belief whole-heartedly. By spelling out what is expected, you reduce stress that is caused by role ambiguity and help staff focus on activities that are important. The net result is lower stressed, task driven, highly productive people.

Part of an effective orientation is taking the time to ensure that the employee can do the basic tasks. It is important to build first upon the similar tasks, then master them prior to moving on.

Employee orientation is not difficult, nor does it consume a lot of time if done right. The reality is that if done correctly, the process can save a tremendous amount of time over the long haul.

A poorly planned or non-existent orientation can quickly undo all the previous efforts of recruiting and selection into one more person travelling through the "revolving door" of personnel. Turnover can be greatly reduced by a well-thought-out orientation program. A well-planned and executed orientation will result in fewer mistakes and a better understanding of what is expected. This should lead to improved customer service, higher productivity and improved employee relations. Everyone wins—you, the employee, the organization, and most of all the real bosses of any company, your customers or clients.

Given human nature, we often tend to imitate what we have experienced. If you received a good orientation in the past, chances are you will conduct your orientation in a similar manner. If your orientation was poor, this chapter can help develop a positive orientation program.

How Well Have You Done in the Past?

Think for a moment about the last few employees your organization hired, then honestly answer the questions below.

	Employee 1	Employee 2	Employee 3
Name:	_____	_____	_____
1. How long has each employee been on board?	_____	_____	_____
2. Do you think the employee was made to feel welcome?	Yes No	Yes No	Yes No
3. Do you think the employee regrets his/her decision to join your organization?	Yes No	Yes No	Yes No
4. Was the employee productive within a short period of time?	Yes No	Yes No	Yes No

5. Did your organization have a planned orientation program?	Yes No	Yes No	Yes No
6. If you had been in the employee's place, would you have been satisfied with the orientation?	Yes No	Yes No	Yes No
7. Did I routinely take time to get to know the employee?	Yes No	Yes No	Yes No
8. Our company had an employee handbook which was kept up-to-date.	Yes No	Yes No	Yes No
9. Welcoming events were scheduled to help new employees get acquainted.	Yes No	Yes No	Yes No
10. Publicity about the employee was routinely circulated.	Yes No	Yes No	Yes No
11. New employees had the opportunity to ask questions when they didn't understand something.	Yes No	Yes No	Yes No

Circle the number that best overall describes the orientation these employees received.

1	2	3	4	5
Poor	Needs Improvement	Not Sure	Good	The Best

Planning the Orientation Program

By failing to plan, you are planning to fail. This old adage relates to many business applications but holds especially true for the Orientation Program. This section will cover four key areas to ensure that your orientation program is successful. They are:

1. Reinforce Job Decision;
2. Review Performance Expectations;
3. Prepare for Training; and
4. Make Them Feel Welcome.

Reinforce Job Decision

Orientation is a great way to allow the new employees to confirm that they have made a wise choice in applying and accepting a position in your organization. It is highly probable that your new employees applied for other positions besides this one. To reduce the incidence of "Buyers Remorse" (the employees second-guessing their decision), the employer can use the orientation period to reinforce the job decision of the employees.

Review Performance Expectations

Role ambiguity—the condition of staff not knowing what is expected of them— is one of the highest causes of on-the-job stress and is often cited as a primary reason for high turnover. Staff need realistic expectations of what will be required of them while on the job. The initial expectations that are communicated to the new hire have a tremendous impact on the employee's performance. If you have high quality performance and this message is well communicated by both words and actions, you will greatly increase the chances of getting a high level of performance from your staff. On the other hand, if you fail to communicate your high expectations, it is very likely that you will receive low performance.

Prepare for Training

Orientation provides an opportunity to start the employee on the right track. A well-planned orientation program will set the stage for all training and development that follows. During the orientation process the skills needed to perform the basic job can be taught. Without the benefit of a progressive orientation an employee is left on his/her own to figure things out for him/herself. This method is impersonal and time-consuming, as well as inefficient. Employees lacking essential information or receiving incorrect or misleading information can learn/develop bad habits. When the stage is set by giving proper direction, clear tasks and specific information, a new hire will be more receptive to training and will make fewer costly errors.

Make Them Feel Welcome

How would you treat a client who was considering purchasing $15,000 of goods from your organization? Chances are you would treat him/her like royalty. New employees are equally important. Set a positive first impression—roll out the red carpet. Here is a good question; why is it that most companies reward people that leave by giving "going away" parties and are neutral when new staff come onboard? Would it not be more beneficial to celebrate the arrival of new staff? An easy way to provide such a welcome is to designate a room and time to invite selected employees to meet the new hire and enjoy coffee and doughnuts.

Publicizing the hiring decision is another way to make the employee feel welcome. There are two primary ways to publicize a hiring decision, internal and external. Internally, an announcement memo could be sent to all appropriate staff, or an article could be written about the new hire for the company newsletter. External publicity can be in the form of a press release with photo in the business section of the local newspaper or trade journals.

It is important that the organization convey to the employee that they are pleased that he/she joined the organization. It is also a good idea to remind the new hire that help is available and any questions or concerns that he/she might have will be dealt with. Do everything in your power to ensure that the new employee feels welcome.

Seven Reminders for a Successful Orientation

1. Devote as much time as possible on the first day to the new employee.
2. Make initial contact with new hire and review orientation schedule prior to assigning new employee to someone else.
3. A breakfast meeting is a unique and relaxing way to welcome your new hire.
4. Be on time: failure to do so sends the message that tardiness is acceptable.
5. Avoid interruption during orientation meetings.
6. Devote l00% of your attention to the employee.
7. Have an overview session with new hire and representative from other departments. Allow new employee to see the "big picture." Some of the areas that should be covered at this point are:
    a. What is the responsibility of each department?
    b. Who reports to whom?
    c. With which departments will the new hire most frequently interact?
    d. What are the major projects that each department is involved with?
    e. What barriers do people encounter on a regular basis?

Sample Orientation Schedule
Week 1

Monday (day 1)

8:30 – 9:30	Breakfast meeting (review orientation schedule).
9:45 – 10:15	Review company history.
10:15 – 12:00	Tour facility and introduce to co-workers.
1:00 – 2:00	Required paperwork.
2:00 – 2:30	Explain system for office supplies.
2:30 – 3:00	Discuss job description.
3:00 – 3:30	Review performance appraisal system.
3:30 – 4:30	Review company policies and procedures.
4:30 – 4:40	Assign first job task.
4:40 – 5:00	Review day.

Tuesday (day 2)

9:00 – 9:45	Roland Jackson, Account Manager.
11:00 – 11:45	Sally Jones, Advertising Coordinator.
1:30 – 2:00	Daren Simpson, Finance Department.
3:00 – 3:45	Russell Miller, Operations Director.
4:45 – 5:00	Meet with supervisor.

Wednesday (day 3)

9:00 – 9:45	Parker Johnson, Research and Development.
10:30 – 11:00	Cheryl Fontaine, Purchasing.
12:00 – 1:00	Lunch with Susan Carson, Personnel Manager.
3:00 – 3:30	Sam Nordick, Legal Department.
4:45 – 5:00	Meet with supervisor.

Thursday (day 4)

Employee shadows management and performs assigned tasks under supervision.

Friday (day 5)

9:00–10:00	Write a short report on operations experience, including observations, suggestions, and questions.
10:00–4:00	Continue work on first assignment.
4:00–4:30	Receive additional assignments.
4:30–5:00	Review first week on the job with supervisor.

Company History

Normally it is a good idea to provide each new hire background information on how the company got started. The goal is to give new employees a sense of identity with the organization. How did it get to where it is today? Each new hire should have a sense of how the past paved the way for what is happening today. When well presented, a company history will reinforce the decision that joining your company was the best possible choice. Some large organizations have developed slide shows or videos designed to show the company's story. Regardless of how the company history is illustrated, the main point to cover is that each employee feels as if they are a direct part of the company's future.

An organization's history should include the following points:

1. Parent company (if applicable);
2. Official company name;
3. What the name represents;
4. Organizational mission;
5. Company philosophy;
6. Notable achievements;
7. Date founded;
8. Founder(s);
9. Company's original size;
10. Current size;
11. Original product(s)/service(s);
12. Current product(s)/service(s); and
13. Future goals

Doing the Walk-A-Bout

Shortly after starting work, the new hire should be taken on what I call the walk-a-bout. This is a tour of the workplace. This tour provides an insider's view of the inner workings of the company. During the tour, be sure to spend time where other members of the new employee's team are located. Take time to introduce the new employee to each person.

"WALK-A-BOUT" Checklist

Check off each item you need to include on your tour of the workplace. Add any others not on the list:

_____ Office area	_____ Cafeteria
_____ Co-workers	_____ Executive Offices
_____ Secretay	_____ Restricted areas
_____ Map of facility	_____ Copy machine
_____ Stairs	_____ Supply area
_____ Elevators	_____ Receptionist
_____ Fire exits	_____ Word processing centre
_____ Mailroom	_____ Files
_____ Vending	_____ Break area
_____ Restrooms	_____ Storage
_____ Parking lots	_____ Conference room

Required Paperwork

Sometime during the first day it is important to have the new employee complete the necessary paperwork for payroll, health benefits, and other items. This is the time to make sure all loose ends are completed. If an employee application is not on file, get one processed. If the employee needs an I.D. card or a key to gain access to the building, have one available.

Although these paperwork items may seem trivial, they can cause real problems later if not taken care of now. Otherwise, it may be necessary to explain why the employee's first check is late or why a family member's visit to the doctor wasn't covered by insurance.

Job Description

During the first day the new hire should receive a copy of his/her job description. Take time to answer any questions.

Cover the following areas:

1. Expectation of job performance;
2. Responsibilities and duties;
3. Priorities; and
4. Training needed to do job.

A complete job description will describe how the employee's duties contribute to the success of the department and the company.

JOB DESCRIPTION

Job Title: _____

Division: _____

Department: _____

Title of Supervisor: _____

Date Last Reviewed: _____

Job Summary: (Briefly describe the purpose of this job, what is done and how.)

_____
_____
_____
_____
_____

Results: (Describe the expected results achieved from having this job performed.)

_____
_____
_____
_____
_____

What is the most difficult/demanding part of this job?

_____
_____
_____
_____
_____

The experience that is required to do this job is:

_____
_____
_____
_____
_____

The qualifications and/or training that are required for this job are:

_____
_____
_____
_____
_____

(Instructions: Divide the position into three key areas of responsibility. Each area of responsibility should be divided into one-to-five principle duties. List the knowledge and skills required for each duty. Also include the equipment and tools required for this position.

1. **RESPONSIBILITY:** _____
   Approximate % of time: _____

Duties:	**Knowledge and Skills Required:**
• _____	• _____
• _____	• _____
• _____	• _____
• _____	• _____
• _____	• _____
Equipment & Tools Required:	**Knowledge and Skills Required:**
• _____	• _____
• _____	• _____
• _____	• _____
• _____	• _____
• _____	• _____

2. **RESPONSIBILITY:** _____
   Approximate % of time: _____

Duties:	Knowledge and Skills Required:
• _____	• _____
• _____	• _____
• _____	• _____
• _____	• _____
• _____	• _____
Equipment & Tools Required:	**Knowledge and Skills Required:**
• _____	• _____
• _____	• _____
• _____	• _____
• _____	• _____
• _____	• _____

3. **RESPONSIBILITY:** _____
   Approximate % of time: _____

Duties:	Knowledge and Skills Required:
• _____	• _____
• _____	• _____
• _____	• _____
• _____	• _____
• _____	• _____
Equipment & Tools Required:	**Knowledge and Skills Required:**
• _____	• _____
• _____	• _____
• _____	• _____
• _____	• _____
• _____	• _____

PREFERRED PERSONALITY PROFILE

Strengths—On the job, individuals *strong* in this dimension tend to be good at:

_____ _____
_____ _____
_____ _____
_____

Individuals who score *low* in the dimension tend to have difficulty in the above areas.

Difficulties—On the job, individuals *strong* in this dimension can also tend to be:

_____ _____
_____ _____
_____ _____
_____ _____

Organization Chart

An employee can get a feel for the "big picture" if presented a copy of the organization chart. This chart should clearly outline the various departments and (the) people staffing them. Employees should at a glance be able to see where their job fits and what the working relationships are among the various departments.

Some companies have drawn out their organizational charts, including pictures of the person holding the position on display in the staff room for everyone to see. This non-traditional approach helps the new employee place names and positions to faces.

Assign First Job Task

New employees are eager to demonstrate their skills and to prove to management that they made a sound hiring decision. Wise managers capitalize on this energy and get the new hire actively involved in work assignments as soon as possible. Many supervisors make the mistake of not assigning a new hire a specific task on the first day. Instead, new employees are often handed stacks of paper and policy manuals. The result of this is that the new hire becomes overwhelmed with data and quickly starts to lose interest and energy.

Orientation Checklist

The items listed below should be covered during new employee orientation.

Required Paperwork
Employee File:

- ___ application blank
- ___ resume & cover letter
- ___ reference checks
- ___ employee benefits
- ___ TD-1 form
- ___ non-competing agreement (if applicable)
- ___ insurance forms
- ___ ID card and keys issued
- ___ selection tests results
- ___ post-interview checklist

Things to Cover:

- ___ Tour of work area & building
- ___ Introduction to co-workers
- ___ Parking
- ___ Time off
- ___ Vacations/holidays
- ___ Dress/appearance/uniforms
- ___ Mail/telephone procedures
- ___ Probation period
- ___ Sick pay
- ___ Employee discounts
- ___ Personal use of equipment
- ___ Job description
- ___ Organization chart
- ___ Hours/work schedule
- ___ Pay rate/paydays
- ___ Incentive plan
- ___ Operations manuals
- ___ Company policies
- ___ Company history
- ___ Office supplies
- ___ Company publications
- ___ Employee Handbook
- ___ Recreation activities
- ___ Confidentiality

Prepare for the New Employee's Arrival By:

1. Preparing a written orientation plan.
2. Designating a work area (office, desk, etc.).
3. Arrange for office supplies.
4. Prepare required paperwork.
5. Keep schedule open to meet with new hire.
6. Arrange breakfast meeting.
7. Schedule staff orientation meetings.
8. Prepare welcoming get-together.
9. Prepare first job assignment.
10. Obtain copies of manuals, policies, etc.

PULLING OUT THE RED CARPET 15

Name _____ **Department** _____
          Last   First   Middle

Date of Birth _____ **Date of Hire** _____ **Clock Number** _____

Social Insurance Number _____ **Sick Days Due** _____ **Vacation Time Due** _____

19___

Employee Attendance Record

	1	2	3	4	5	6	7	8	9	10	11	12	13	14	15	16	17	18	19	20	21	22	23	24	25	26	27	28	29	30	31
Jan																															
Feb																														▨	▨
Mar																															▨
Apr																															▨
May																															
Jun																															▨
Jul																															
Aug																															▨
Sept																														▨	
Oct																															▨
Nov																															
Dec																															

Absence Summary

A	AO	D	DF	H	J	LA	SF	SS	V	X	EO

A = Accident on Duty   DF = Death in Family   LA = Leave of Absence   V = Vacation
AO = Accident Off Duty   H = Holiday   SF = Sickness in Family X = Unexcused Absence
D = Discipline   J = Jury Duty   SS = Sickness-Self   EO = Excused (Other)

Confidential Employee History

Employee Name	Employment Date	Status			
		☐ Regular	☐ Part Time	☐ Temporary	

Years of Service	1	2	3	4	5	6	7	8	9	10	11	12	13	14	15	16	17	18	19	20	21	22	23	24	25	26

Security Clearance	Level	Date Granted

Payroll Data

Birthdate	Sex	Social Insurance No.	Marital Status	Name of Spouse	No. of Children

Hospital Insurance No.	Medicare Insurance No.

	Date Eligible	Date Joined	Date Withdrawn	Insurance	Date Eligible	Date Joined	Date
Union Status				Life			
Pension Plan				Medical-Self			
Credit Union				Dependent(s)			
				Maj. Med-Self			
				Dependent(s)			

General Information

Address	City	Province	Code	Phone
Address	City	Province	Code	Phone
Address	City	Province	Code	Phone
Address	City	Province	Code	Phone

In Emergency Notify

	Relationship	City	Province	Code	Phone
	Relationship	City	Procince	COde	Phone

Relatives or Friends Employed by This Company

Name	Relationship

Education

Grade School _____ High School _____

University 1 2 3 4 Major _____

Other _____

Special Skills or Training

Termination Record

☐ **Resignation** Date____	Reason
☐ **Dismissal** Date____	Reason
Recommended for Re-Employment ☐ Yes ☐ No	Reason

SAMPLE PERSONNEL POLICY
(taken from a day care facility)

Employment of Staff

The Personnel Committee in conjunction with the program director has the responsibility for hiring staff. Staff members are required to be eighteen years of age or over, have completed Grade XI or equivalent, and must be in good health.

Salaries

All salaries will be reviewed by the Personnel Committee and Finance Committee and recommendations will be brought to the Board for consideration. The salaries paid are based upon qualification and experience. All staff will be paid on the basis of 26 pay periods. Increments will be considered after a 3-month probationary period and on the employee's anniversary date. Mileage will be paid to staff–records must be maintained and an appropriate claim submitted to the Director.

Hours of Work

The normal hours of work will be forty hours weekly, Monday to Friday inclusive. A lunch period of one hour will be granted. Two rest periods, one morning and one afternoon, each of fifteen minutes duration shall be part of the working day.

Overtime
  a. No financial compensation
  b. Time off in lieu
  c. Records maintained
  d. To be taken as soon after as incurred.

Statutory Holidays

All permanent employees shall be granted the following eleven holidays annually with remuneration:

New Year's Day	Canada Day	Civic Holiday
Good Friday	Thanksgiving Day	Boxing Day
Easter Monday	Rememberance Day	Labour Day
Victoria Day	Christmas Day	

If a holiday falls on Saturday or Sunday, a day in lieu of the holiday will be given each full-time employee. This must be taken within thirty working days and is to be arranged with the Administrator.

Vacation

All full-time employees with 6 months service shall receive one week (5 working days) vacation with pay annually; twelve months service shall receive two weeks (10 working days) vacation annually with pay; three years service shall receive three weeks (15 working days) vacation with pay annually; five years service shall receive 4 weeks maximum vacation with pay annually with stipulation that these four weeks will not be taken consecutively. All vacation must be taken within the calendar year January 1 to December 31. Vacation for part time workers will be calculated accordingly.

Sick Leave

Employees may accumulate up to one and one-half sick days per month to a maximum of 15 days per year with a carry over of no more than 15 days in any given year. If absent from his/her duties for five consecutive days, a medical certificate must be obtained. When a staff member is ill, he/she must advise, by telephone, the Director or an employee designated by the Director one hour prior to the beginning of her regular work day and report again every day thereafter for the duration of the illness.

Leave of Absence

Leaves of absence will be considered for those wishing to continue their studies in Day Care. Leave of absence for other special circumstances such as death in family, serious illness, pregnancy, conferences, shall be considered at the discretion of the Personnel Committee and the Board of Directors. This leave of absence shall be without pay, nor shall vacation and/or sick leave be accumulated during this leave.

Compassionate Leave

When death occurs to a member of the immediate family of an employee, such employee shall be granted compassionate leave with pay, for a period not to exceed five days. The members of the immediate family are employee's spouse, mother, father, brothers, sisters, sons and daughters.

Extended family shall be granted one compassionate day of leave. This leave may be extended at the discretion of the Director in consultation with the Board Chairman and/or Personnel Chairman.

Time Off For Appointments

Time off for appointments will be granted at the discretion of the director.

Termination of Employment

An employee shall forward a letter to the Personnel Committee or Director not less than ten working days prior to the effective date of termination.

Dismissal of Staff

The Administrator, in conjunction with the Personnel Committee, may suspend any staff member immediately for insubordination, immorality, i.e.: irresponsibility. The employee has the right to appeal, within five days, first to the Personnel Committee, and if not satisfied, to the Board. Such persons need only write or telephone the Personnel Committee chairman to request a meeting. The Personnel Committee, in conjunction with the Board of Directors, has the responsibility of disciplining and dismissal of all staff. The responsibility of staff training and disciplining may be delegated to the Administrator.

Staff Evaluation and Training

The Administrator and Chairman of the Personnel Committee, with the assistance of Early Childhood Education specialists, will continually evaluate staff program, facilities, and all areas of the operation, as it relates to staff. The Personnel Committee has the responsibility for suggesting Staff Training.

Medicals

The Day Care Act requires that each employee have a yearly medical exam stating that he/she is free of communicable diseases.

CONCLUSION

Even after a comprehensive orientation, new employees seldom perform satisfactorily. Thus the need for employee training. Chapter Two deals with the issues surrounding training and developing your key resource . . . your staff.

Chapter Two

TRAINING AND DEVELOPING YOUR KEY RESOURCE... YOUR STAFF

    The importance of training has been increasing in our society for a number of reasons. The first of these is the grand developments in technology that have been affecting the workplace. As jobs become more complex, higher levels of training and education will be needed for the work force to be able to perform these jobs. This developing of self must take place when entering the job market as well as on a continuous basis in order to not only advance to higher positions, but also to maintain the same job. Also, due to higher levels of automation many of the unskilled jobs have disappeared or are disappearing. If employees are expecting to remain in the job market, they are forced to train themselves to deal with new processes and production techniques.

    Another very practical reason for training is to increase profits by increasing the productivity of workers. Any new knowledge that the employee can gain will improve job performance and thereby increase profits. Training can also cut down costs by decreasing accidents through safety training programs on the job. The costs of accidents, injuries, damaged equipment and lost company time can be very high.

    Manpower can be looked at through a skill inventory system where files are kept on the entire work force. These files are effective in keeping management of the firm aware of the skills and abilities of its work force, and in keeping management aware of where there are deficiencies which can be corrected with a training program. By keeping these files updated, we can also be aware of the career goals of the individuals in the firm and which paths are open to them in regards to promotions or transfers in the near future.

In order to keep the training process up-to-date we must keep these analysis programs going on a continuous basis. They must be reviewed constantly and changed in the light of the company advances and discoveries.

SKILLS INVENTORY

PART I (to be completed by personnel department)

Employee name _____

Employee number _____

Job title_____ Experience _____ years

Age _____ Years with A.B.C. Company _____

Other jobs held:

• with A.B.C. Company:

Title: _____ from _____ to _____

Title: _____ from _____ to _____

Title: _____ from _____ to _____

• elsewhere:

Title: _____ from _____ to _____

Title: _____ from _____ to _____

PART II (to be completed by employee)

Special Skills: List below any skills you possess even if they are not used in your present job.

skills:_____

_____

_____

_____

machine & tools:_____

_____

_____

_____

Duties: Briefly describe your present duties: _____

_____

_____

_____

Education: Briefly describe your education and training background:

	Years Completed	Year Graduated	Certification
High School:	_____	_____	_____
Post Secondary:	_____	_____	_____
Job Training:	_____	_____	_____
Special Courses:	_____	_____	_____

PART III (to be completed by personnel department with supervisory input)

Evaluation of Employee

Overall: _____
_____
_____

Overall readiness for position: _____
_____

To what job(s): _____

Comments: _____
_____
_____

Current deficiencies: _____
_____
_____

Employee Signature: _____

Date: _____

Supervisor Signature: _____

Date: _____

Is It a Training Problem?

Training is often used as the answer to all of our daily work problems. If an individual is not performing up to standard, it is very easy to assume that "training" will improve the employee's performance.

Before you call anything a "training problem," think for a minute. Training may not be the solution to your problem.

For example, a driver may constantly roll through stop signs rather than stop completely. He knows he should stop, but he has never received a traffic ticket. Does this person need training in how to stop at a stop sign? No, he needs to get a ticket each time he rolls through the stop sign.

Similarly, a bank teller may know how to balance cash properly but begins to make many errors. Before jumping to the conclusion that the teller needs more training, the teller's supervisor should investigate to find out why the teller is not performing up to standard. The teller's problem may be lack of motivation rather than lack of training.

A simple way to determine if a problem is a training problem is to ask yourself, "Could the employee do the job if his/her life depended on it?"

If the answer is yes . . . then investigate to find the real cause of the problem. Eg: poor supervision, increased workload, new systems, lack of motivation.

If the answer is no . . . then training may be the answer.

The Four Step Method of Instruction

Before you can begin to instruct an employee, you have to be prepared. Select a training time when you will be able to devote all your efforts and concentration upon the instruction and when all equipment, people and other resources are easily available. Make a timetable of how much knowledge you expect your trainee to have and by what date. Break the new job down into the important steps and pick out the key points.

The training session should be broken into "bite-size" chunks that the trainee can handle.

The "4P" approach is easy to remember and follow.

- Step 1   Preparation
- Step 2   Presentation
- Step 3   Practice
- Step 4   Performance

Preparation
Get the trainee ready to learn new ideas and information.
- State the objective.
- Tell where the job fits into the overall picture.
- Make the employee feel at ease.
- Associate trainee's past experiences with the new task to be learned.
- Introduce the trainee to new tools, materials, equipment and words.
- Explain why it is important to do the job properly.
- Explain the consequences of doing the job incorrectly.

Presentation
Demonstrate by showing and telling how the job should be done.
- Present one point at a time.
- Do so slowly and clearly.
- Relate the job to the trainee's past experience.
- If it is a mechanical operation, make sure you and the trainee face the same direction.
- Emphasize the key points and the sequence of learning.
- Limit details—the average person can remember only seven points in one lesson.
- Tell why things are done—this helps trainees remember.

Practice
Have the trainee do the job under your direct supervision.
- Have trainee do the job, one point at a time, telling you in advance what has to be done at each step.
- Have the trainee explain why the task is done.
- Let trainee ask questions, but help him/her to recall on his/her own.
- Anticipate possible errors.
- Have trainee correct any errors instantly.
- Insure that trainee understands. Ask questions about each step that can not be answered "yes" or "no." Use Who, What, Where, When, Why and How questions.
- Have trainee repeat the job until you know he/she knows.

Performance

Have the trainee do the job under normal work conditions.
- Tell the trainee what and how much to do.
- Tell the trainee where to go for assistance and advice.
- Check frequently.
- Taper off supervision gradually.
- Use positive reinforcement as appropriate.

Here is an example of how the Four Step Method of Instruction works:

Teaching a Teller Trainee to Sell Canadian Money Orders

1. **Preparation**
- Find out what the trainee knows about selling Canadian money orders.
- Show the trainee a money order and explain its purpose.
- Explain that money orders can be sold for amounts up to and including $1,000.
- Explain that money orders should be "protectographed."
- Show the trainee the protectographing machine and describe its purpose.
- Explain the importance of protectographing the right amount on the money order.
- Explain what could happen if the wrong amount is printed on the money order or the wrong portion of the money order given to the customer.

2. **Presentation**
- Show the trainee where the money orders are kept.
- Explain the importance of keeping money orders locked up.
- Explain and show how to protectograph the amount on the money order.
- Explain why and show how customers must fill in the date, name of payee and name of sender on the money order.
- Explain why and show how to cancel a money order.
- Explain why you should never destroy a money order.
- Explain why and show how service charges are collected.

- Explain why and show how the portions of the money order are processed.
- Explain why and show how to collect and process the payment for the money order.

3. Practice
- Have the trainee go through the process of preparing a money order.
- Have the trainee explain and show each step of the process.
- Correct any misunderstandings immediately.
- Question the trainee until you are sure he/she knows how and when to sell money orders.
- Have the trainee cancel a money order and describe why and when this should be done.
- Have the trainee practice with different examples until you know he/she understands.

4. Performance
- Have the trainee sell money orders as part of his/her regular teller duties.
- Tell the trainee to go to the Teller Trainer in cases of difficulty.
- Check the trainee's work carefully and frequently.
- Correct any errors immediately.
- Give appropriate recognition for a job well done.

Setting Training Objectives

Before you start training, you must establish your training objectives. In other words, you must determine and explain to your trainees what they will be able to do after being trained and why it is important. If you do not know where you are going, you and your trainee are not likely to get there.

You will be able to establish your training objectives when you have decided:
- what you want the trainee to be able to do when training is over;
- what performance standards the trainee will be expected to meet;
- what the trainee must know versus what can be looked up or referred to a supervisor;

- what information the trainee needs in order to perform as desired;
- what the trainee must know during the first few weeks on the job (needs to know) versus what will be learned after being on the job awhile (nice to know).

Training objectives should always be stated in terms that are realistic, obtainable and measurable.

Training Feedback

In every training session, you should give your trainee specific and immediate feedback on his/her performance. You must let your trainee know his/her particular strengths and weaknesses.

By giving your trainees specific feedback on their responses for actions, you increase the chance that they will perform correctly in the future.

- If a response or action is correct and you let the trainee know immediately why it was correct, you have provided positive reinforcement.
- If a response is incorrect and you let the trainee know immediately why it was incorrect and how it should be done correctly, you have provided negative reinforcement. After giving negative feedback, always provide your trainee with an immediate opportunity to practice the task the proper way.

By providing both positive and negative reinforcements at the appropriate time and place you will increase the chances for getting correct performance in the future, which is what training is all about.

Some trainers are reluctant to correct a trainee. They praise good performance, but overlook mistakes because they do not want to discourage trainees. They hope the trainee will improve with time.

However, this attitude may actually hinder the learning more than anything else. When trainees learn to do something incorrectly, it is very difficult to relearn it properly.

People need to know where they have failed, as well as where they have succeeded. Mistakes must be corrected before they become a habit. How the correcting is done is crucial.

Plan your feedback sessions so you can discuss things privately. Provide the negative feedback in a positive and constructive manner. This will increase the chances that the trainee will perform successfully in the future.

When correcting trainee responses or actions, trainers should focus on the job being done, not on the person. For example, it is better to say, "You have been late for work eight times this month," rather than, "You have a poor attitude to work schedules."

Evaluation

Training is not complete unless you and your trainee evaluate the success of the training. If it is worthwhile to undertake training, it is equally worthwhile to find out what has been accomplished.

Evaluating a trainee's performance is not difficult to do. If the objectives are properly set at the beginning, they will tell you what the trainee should be able to do at the end of the training period. Evaluation, then, is finding out if the trainee can actually do what the objectives state.

If the trainee accomplishes the objectives, then the training has been successful.

Evaluation becomes difficult when objectives are not stated correctly in the first place. Look at these objectives:

1. At the end of this course, the employee will have a good understanding of loan granting.
2. At the end of this course, the employee will be able to correctly complete a term plan application based on information obtained in a client interview.

How would you evaluate trainee performance for the first objective? Everyone will probably have a different opinion. The test for this item could range from "Being able to list the different types of loans available" to "Being able to establish interest rates on loan."

The word "understanding" is confusing. You do not know what the trainee must do to demonstrate "understanding."

For the second example, there is no confusion. Everyone, including the trainee, knows what must be done to accomplish the objectives.

You can see how important it is to set clear and measurable objectives.

How to Evaluate

Evaluating a change in a trainee's knowledge, skill or attitude can be done in several ways:

- performance tests where trainees must actually perform the skill.
- oral or written tests of trainee's knowledge.
- interviews with trainees.
- observing trainees on the job.

When evaluating a trainee's performance, make sure you evaluate them only on what you have asked them to learn.

For example, suppose you are given the following objective for training:

"To be able to change a car tire, while observing all safety precautions and using the equipment in the trunk of the car."

For weeks you practice changing tires under all weather conditions and on all types of roads. When the trainer comes to evaluate your efforts, you are asked to complete the following test items:

1. Diagram the parts of the tire.
2. List the different types of tires.
3. Inspect a tire for possible defects.

What would your reaction be? Right, the trainer cannot find out if you know how to change a tire unless the trainer watches you change a tire.

How would you feel if you had been told to learn one thing and were then tested on another? You would probably be angry and rightly so!

When evaluating your trainees, remember:

1. Make sure your objectives for training are clear and specific.
   Make sure both you and the trainee know what is expected of the trainee upon completion of the training.
2. Evaluate your trainees only on what you have asked them to learn in the objectives.

Follow Up

Training should be an ongoing process in a branch or department. Trainees should be followed up on after training is completed to see if they are meeting the performance standards.

This follow up can be done in several ways.
- Formal testing of the material presented.
- Interviewing and observing the trainee perform on the job.
- Interviewing the trainee's supervisor to see how well the trainee is meeting performance standards.

By following up on your trainees, you will also get feedback on your ability to train people.

Assessing Training Needs

In the assessment of training needs, you must seek to answer the questions, "Who, if anyone, needs training?" and, "What training do they need?" These questions appear simple, but in order to obtain good answers, we must look at various different factors within the organization. Organizational analysis is a study of the entire organization. This includes its objectives, its resources and the ways in which they attempt to reach their objectives with their given resources.

The first step in organizational analysis is to obtain a clear understanding of both short-term and long-term goals. Long-term goals are generally established for the entire company, while short-term goals meet specific targets and strategies for achieving these long-term goals. This process is continuous due to the constantly changing nature of the business environment.

The second step to organizational analysis is an inventory of the company's attempts to meet the goals through its manpower and physical components. In attempting to look at training, of course, the focus should be on the human resource spectrum.

The final step to look at is the organizational climate. This includes the socialization of the employees in the various aspects of work. Since this process is a learned one, training may be designed to make changes in this climate to improve the work environment.

Job analysis involves a careful study of jobs to determine the specific needs of training. This method requires a collection of data about what tasks constitute a job, how they are to be performed, and what behavior the worker needs in order to perform satisfactorily. These job analyses are easier at lower level jobs in the organization, and become much more complex as the individual moves to higher levels in the organization.

Labor analysis focuses on the individual in a given job, rather than the job itself. The first thing we must observe in the individual is whether performance is adequate or if training is needed. We need to know if employees are capable of the needed training, and the specific area in which they require training.

CONFIDENTIAL

TRAINING NEEDS ASSESSMENT QUESTIONNAIRE

Company Name: _____

Address: _____

_____

_____

_____

Phone Number: _____ Fax Numbers: _____

Contact's Name: _____

Title: _____

Owner(s) Name: _____

Years in Business: _____

Years Owned by Present Owner(s): _____

Questionnaire Completed by: _____

Date: _____

Selecting Staff For Training

There are, unfortunately, times when not all staff have the option of participating in training. It may be determined that not everyone on the staff requires the training in question. In these circumstances, the strong interpersonal skills of the manager/owner are called upon to identify training participants without bruising egos and hurting feelings. Those selected may feel either pleased or "picked on." Those not chosen may feel slighted or anxious. There are no absolute techniques for handling these situations, but sensitivity and other staff development options can go a long way toward maintaining harmonious relations.

When the determining factor in staff selection for training is funding or substitute coverage, choices may be made on the basis of interest. If many staff members express interest in receiving the training, choice by lottery is another option. Personnel must be informed about the selection criteria. If all have a sense that they are being treated fairly and other learning opportunities are provided, then most staff will have a positive response to training.

If some staff must be singled out for training, a resentful or fearful response alone may interfere and create an attitude not conducive to learning. The manager must calm, reassure, and support the staff members who have special learning needs.

> The following section will help us get started on determining whether or not there exists a real need for training. Sometimes research has shown us that the solution lies elsewhere other than training. A major reason for doing a Needs Assessment is to define the problems for which training is the only and best way to achieve a solution.

Selected Sources of Information

- Owner/Owners
- Board of Directors
- Executive Team
- Supervisors
- Employers
- Customers
- Policies
- Laws
- Management Practices
- Budgets
- Financial Results
- Annual Plans
- Schedules
- Procedures
- Equipment/Hardware
- Systems/Software
- Performance Appraisals
- Productivity Reports
- Departments
- Work Groups
- Informal Cliques
- Individuals Affected by Needs Assessment Results
- Physical Environment
- Specifications
- Current Courses

Use the following worksheet to list the most important individuals to whom you can turn for support, straight answers and relevant commentary.

Key Informers

Name	Organization	Address	Telephone

(Add more pages as needed.)

In order to answer whether or not training is the most appropriate solution, this Training Needs Assessment will answer the following 12 key questions and a series of sub-questions.

1. What is the performance discrepancy?
   - What is the difference between what is being done and what is expected?
   - What is my evidence?
   - How reliable is my evidence?
2. Is the discrepancy important?
   - Why?
   - What happens if we do nothing?
   - Is it worth making better?
3. Is it a lack of skill?
   - Could the performers do it if their lives depended on doing the job correctly?
   - Are present skills at least adequate?
4. Were they able to perform successfully in the past?
   - Have they forgotten?
   - Do they know it's still expected of them?
5. Is the needed skill used frequently?
   - Do they get regular feedback on how well they are/are not doing?
   - Exactly how do they find out how they are doing?
   - How do they view the way they are told?
6. Is there a simpler way to do the job?
   - Would job aids clear up the problems?
   - Can they learn/relearn by watching others?
   - Can the job be changed some way?
7. Do they have what it takes to do the job?
   - Is the physical and/or mental potential there?
   - Are they overqualified?

8. Is the desired performance inadvertently being punished?
    - What's in it for the performer to do it right?
    - Is doing it somehow self-punishing?
    - Is there some pressure not to perform?
9. Is not doing the job rewarding in some way?
    - Is there some reward for doing it wrong?
    - Does doing it wrong draw attention?
    - What rewards the wrong performance now?
    - Do performers worry less or get less tired if they do less work?
10. Does doing the job right really matter?
    - Is there a favorable outcome for doing?
    - Is there an unfavorable outcome for not doing?
    - Is there self-pride in doing? Not doing?
    - Is there any status or lack of it connected with the job?
11. Are there obstacles to performing?
    - Do they know what is expected?
    - Do they know when it is expected?
    - Are there too many competing demands?
    - Are time and tools available?
    - Are there tradition, policy, or ego barriers?
    - Is the job physically a mess?
12. What are the limits on possible solutions?
    - Are there solutions that would be considered unacceptable to the organizations?
    - Do key decision makers have preferred solutions?
    - Are there solutions beyond the organization's time and money resources?

Section 1 Overview of Organization

This organization is a: General Business Description:

    ☐ Government Agency   ☐ Manufacturing
    ☐ Association   ☐ Wholesale
    ☐ Corporation   ☐ Retail
    ☐ Partnership   ☐ Service
    ☐ Tourism/Hospitality

Our Principal Products or Services are: _____
_____
_____
_____

We have _____ locations/branches.

We are located in the following provinces: _____
_____
_____
_____

States: _____
_____
_____

Countries: _____
_____
_____

The current number of employees working for your business?

(Interviewer check)

    ☐ 0–9 employees   ☐ Full-time vs. Part-time
    ☐ 10–19 employees   ☐ Full_____
    ☐ 20–49 employees   ☐ Part_____
    ☐ 50–99 employees   ☐ Seasonal_____
    ☐ 100–199 employees
    ☐ Over 200

The general education level of your employees

(Interviewer check)
- ☐ less than grade 9
- ☐ grades 10–13
- ☐ some post-secondary
- ☐ trade certificate or diploma
- ☐ university degree

Organization gross revenue range is:
- ☐ $0–99,000
- ☐ 100,000–499,000
- ☐ 500,000–999,000
- ☐ 1,000,000–2,999,000
- ☐ 3,000,000–9,999,000
- ☐ 10,000,000–49,000,000
- ☐ 50,000,000+

Our key concerns are:
- ☐ Can't find good people
- ☐ Can't manage the people we have
- ☐ Not enough time
- ☐ Not enough profits
- ☐ Not enough customers
- ☐ All of the above
- ☐ Others:

Who are your primary competitors? _____
_____
_____
_____

What are your competitors' major strengths? _____
_____
_____
_____

What are their major weaknesses? _____
_____
_____
_____

What are your organization's key strengths? _____
_____
_____

What are your organization's areas most in need of improvement? ____
_____
_____
_____

What is the organization's vision or mission statement? _____
_____
_____
_____

What are the original primary objectives? _____
_____
_____
_____

What is your management philosophy? _____
_____
_____
_____

What are your organization's short term goals?
  A. Corporate: (New location, environment, etc.) _____
     _____
     _____
     _____

  B. Sales: (New Products/Services) _____
     _____
     _____
     _____

  C. Other: _____
     _____
     _____
     _____

List and describe any prior training program(s) in the past and indicate if they have been successful or not. _____
_____
_____
_____

List any particular experiences in past training programs that would affect future programs. _____
_____
_____
_____

What new training methods should be considered for the future? _____
_____
_____
_____

Do you have any staff that needs training to fulfill their job responsibilities to the level you feel is acceptable? List them _____
_____
_____
_____

In-House Trainers:

1. Have they had formal training as a trainer?
   ☐ Yes   ☐ No
2. Have they had sufficient experiences that would help them understand the various points of view of the staff they are training?
   ☐ Yes   ☐ No
3. How effective are they as communicators? Do they speak clearly? Are they good listeners? Are they dynamic in their training?
   ☐ Yes   ☐ No
4. Have they taught or trained adult learners before?
   ☐ Yes   ☐ No
5. Are they patient enough to wait for training results?
   ☐ Yes   ☐ No

Section 2   Training and Development

Number of weeks new employees are trained? _____

Number of weeks per annum existing employees receive training? ____

Method(s) of training employees:
- ☐ In-House:
- ☐ Orientation Training
- ☐ On-the-job Training
- ☐ Job Instruction Training
- ☐ Apprentice Training
- ☐ Job Rotation/Cross Training
- ☐ Coaching
- ☐ Audio/Visual based Training
- ☐ Case Study
- ☐ Simulation

External Training:
- ☐ Lecture
- ☐ Role Playing
- ☐ Sensitivity Training
- ☐ Seminar and Conferences
- ☐ Customized Workshops
- ☐ Tapes, Books and Videos

Training Aids:
- ☐ Written Instructions
- ☐ Books/Manuals/Self Directed Workbooks
- ☐ Charts and Graphs
- ☐ Handouts
- ☐ Written Exercises
- ☐ Audio Tapes
- ☐ Films
- ☐ Slides
- ☐ Video Tapes

- ☐ Group Discussion
- ☐ Group Games
- ☐ Observation of Others
- ☐ Small Group Activities

Amount of training budget? _____

Check Your Teaching Stress Level

Directions: We all experience some level in our work and personal lives. Occasionally, however, stress overwhelms us and we exhibit physical, psychological, and behavioral symptoms that are indicators that something is wrong. These symptoms may not be easy for us to see in ourselves, although family, co-workers, and friends may observe changes in us.

Check each answer **True** or **False**.

		True	False
I. Physical Symptoms			
A.	I am always tired.	☐	☐
B.	I am often sick or in pain.	☐	☐
C.	I have regular headaches.	☐	☐
D.	I have recently gained (or lost) a lot of weight.	☐	☐
E.	I have trouble sleeping at night.	☐	☐
F.	When I eat my stomach becomes upset.	☐	☐
G.	I spend a lot of time sleeping.	☐	☐

	True	False
II. Psychological Symptoms		
A. I dislike getting up in the morning.	☐	☐
B. I often feel depressed or sad and do not know why.	☐	☐
C. I feel unattractive.	☐	☐
D. I am dissatisfied with my life.	☐	☐
E. I often feel I would like to escape from my responsibilities.	☐	☐
F. Few people care about me.	☐	☐
G. People cannot get along without me.	☐	☐
III. Behavioral Symptoms		
A. I do not get along with my co-workers.	☐	☐
B. I often argue with members of my family.	☐	☐
C. I have to do most things myself or they will not get done.	☐	☐
D. I have a drink every day to relax.		
E. Drugs make me feel more confident/comfortable with myself.	☐	☐
F. Other people make my life difficult.	☐	☐
G. I have trouble making my needs known to others.	☐	☐

If you check more than two items in any category, your stress level may be too high.

Support Staff Training Needs Analysis

Employee's Name:_____Title:_____

Years on the job:_____Years with organization:_____

The purpose of this training needs analysis is to obtain your opinion about the amount of additional training that the above mentioned person needs in order to be as effective as possible in his/her job.

Please rate each training topic on the following rate:

- 0 Does not apply
- 1 Very little need
- 2 Little need
- 3 Some need
- 4 Considerable need
- 5 Immediate need

Training Topics	Priority	Sources	Comment
Keyboard/Computer			
Business Writing			
Filing/Mail			
Reception			
Telephone			
Customer Service			
Accounting and Financial			
Decision Making			
Problem Solving			
Interpersonal Relations			
Effective Communications			
Time Management			
Stress Management			
Positive Mental Attitude			
Other Topics			

Management Training Needs Analysis

Employee's Name:_____ Title:_____

Years on the job:_____ Years with organization:_____

The purpose of this training needs analysis is to obtain your opinion about the amount of additional training that the above mentioned person needs in order to be as effective as possible in his/her job.

Please rate each training topic on the following rate:

    0   Does not apply
    1   Very little need
    2   Little need
    3   Some need
    4   Considerable need
    5   Immediate need

Training Topics	Priority	Sources	Comment
Team Building			
Leadership			
Train the Trainer			
Positive Discipline			
Positive Mental Attitude			
Professionalism			
Dealing with Difficult People			
Employee Involvement			
Decision Making			
Creative Problem Solving			
Staff Motivation			
Effective Communications			
Performance Appraisals			
Running an Effective Meeting			
Public Speaking			
Effective Presentations			
Writing Job Descriptions			

Training Topics	Priority	Sources	Comment
Cost Control			
Quality Control			
Employee Counseling			
Goal Setting			
Strategic Planning			
Delegating Work			
Employee Scheduling			
Customer Service			
Sales/Sales Management			
Telephone Skills			
Hiring Right Person			
Analyzing and Forecasting Staff Requirements			
Time Management			
Stress Management			
Business Opportunities			
Future Trends			
Negotiating Skills			
Raising Capital			
Managing Information			
Computer Training			
Inventory Management			
Managing/Collecting Receivables			
Financial Analysis			
Cash Flow Management			
Community Marketing			
Franchising			
Exporting			
Importing			
Doing Business with Government			
Others			

Sales and Marketing Training Needs Analysis

Employee's Name:_____Title:_____

Years on the job:_____Years with organization:_____

The purpose of this training needs analysis is to obtain your opinion about the amount of additional training that the above mentioned person needs in order to be as effective as possible in his/her job.

Please rate each training topic on the following rate:

    0   Does not apply
    1   Very little need
    2   Little need
    3   Some need
    4   Considerable need
    5   Immediate need

Training Topics	Priority	Sources	Comment
Stress Management			
Effective Communication			
Time Management			
Prospecting Clients			
Great Openers			
Uncovering Buying Motivators			
Effective Sales Presentations			
Handling Objections			
Closing the Sale			
After Sale Account Building			
Professionalism/Dress			
Telemarketing			
Phone Sales Power			
Positive Mental Attitude			
Networking			
Collecting Money and Keeping Accounts			
Customer Service			

Training Topics	Priority	Sources	Comment
Advertising/Promotion			
Layout and Design			
Merchandising			
Direct Marketing			
Market and Customer Research			
Goal Setting			
Solution Finding			
Decision Making			
Negotiating			
Trade Show Marketing			
Community Marketing			
Publicity			
Others			

Training can be broken into two categories:

1. Internal training
2. External training

Internal training methods include;
1. Orientation training
2. On-the-job training
3. Job instruction training
4. Apprentice training
5. Job rotation/Cross training
6. Coaching
7. Management by objectives
8. Audio-Visual training
9. Case study
10. Simulation

Orientation Training

Orientation training is very essential for a new employee who is entering a company. This is a method where the employee is introduced to his/her job environment, to the people he/she will be working with and to the company policies which will affect him/her in his/her job. This orientation training can be quite extensive in a larger company and can begin with a history of the company, its goals, objectives and the personal touch that the company likes to show its customers. The employee should be put in the charge of a supervisor or a more experienced worker where he will be shown around the department, gradually introduced to people he will work with and shown where the facilities he will work with are located and if necessary, how to use them. This training should begin by giving necessary information to the new employee and providing plenty of opportunities for questions to be asked by and answered for the employee. This basic introduction to the company should be followed by a supervised training of the specific job of the employee.

On-The-Job Training

On-the-job training is most practical because it requires no special space or equipment to undertake. It is cheaper and easier than off-the-job training because the employee produces and earns profits while he/she is learning to do his/her job. On-the-job training allows the new employee to learn exactly what he/she will be expected to perform after his/her training ends. In his booklet, "How Do People Grow in a Business Organization?", Moorhead Wright describes ten principles which have a great significance for development. Principle four states that "a man's development is 90% the result of his experience in his day-to-day work!" This emphasizes the importance of the initial on-the-job training and that a formal program would probably be most successful under the influence of a supervisor who is well aware of the job's demands and techniques.

On-the-job training also allows the socialization process to occur where the employee can become used to the procedures as well as to the personal climate at the workplace. He may at this time meet the people in the organization who will affect his job and who he will be responsible to.

Disadvantages of on-the-job training include the possibility of tying up expensive machinery and slowing down the normal production cycle for those already trained. On-the-job training is generally used for production training and may not be enough for higher level jobs in the hierarchy where higher skill levels and training are needed.

Job Instruction Training

This form of training is used for white-collar and blue-collar workers as well as technicians. This requires a trained instructor, an analysis of the job to be done, a training schedule and a basic knowledge of what the trainee will need to obtain from the training.

The main push for job instruction training began with a program in 1940 in the United States called the *Training Within Industry Program.* This was developed as a defense service to make use of the best potential of all workers in the industry. This policy showed managers that not only was training an everyday tool, but that it was very important to train supervisors in order to obtain the best results in all departments.

In setting up the program, they utilized a lot of the works of Frederick W. Taylor. He discovered by studying managers and workers that many managers were not totally clear in what they wanted from their workers, and that workers were similarly not sure what managers expected from them. Taylor studied the procedures of doing a job and divided the steps into simple movements that he considered important. He attempted to cut down the time spent doing a job and established standards for a better quality of work. In his studies on standardization, he made it easier to train workers because it was more obvious to both managers and trainees what was expected of them. (Kirkpatrick, Donald, *Supervisory Training and Development,* Addison Wesley Publishing Company, Philippines, 1971.)

The method of training employees is now more clear for the supervisor to carry out. The trainee, after being given a statement of the overall purpose of the job, is given a step-by-step demonstration of the job he/she will perform. The trainee is then given a chance to perform the task alone. The trainee practices until he/she reaches a satisfactory level of performance; during this time both the trainee and the trainer may ask questions of the other to make sure there is a proper understanding of the procedure between them. It is important that the skilled trainer be observant of the faults of the trainee so he can stop them before the trainee adopts these faults as habits. The trainer must also check back at some point to make sure the trainee has no new questions and that he/she is maintaining proper performance.

Apprentice Training

Apprentice training can be a formal training where trainees are placed under a supervisor for a specific number of years and at the end automatically become a trainee, or it can be more informal with a volunteer relationship between labour and management. In both of these situations, the trainee is given thorough instruction and experience on the job in the aspects of a skilled trade. As well as job instruction, it is often necessary that the trainee be required to take some formal education at the same time. In order for these programs to work, it is important that the supervisor be committed to the development of the trainee and that there is a periodic evaluation of the trainee's performance. A good apprenticeship program keeps in mind the individual differences in learning aptitudes of the trainers, although many programs today lack the personal touch.

Job Rotation

Job rotation provides the trainee with a series of movements around the company in order to get an overall view of the company. The trainee receives coaching from his/her immediate supervisor in each department in an attempt to acquire knowledge about the interdependencies of the different departments in the company such as finance, marketing and production. In order to be successful, this program must keep in mind the individual capabilities of each trainee and must be flexible enough to allow for these differences. Goals must be set for each movement through the company in order to increase the employee's committment to the total program. These goals can also help the trainee's supervisor monitor progress so he/she can be moved along without delay.

Coaching

Coaching is a relationship between the trainee and supervisor, which is similar to job rotation except that the coach in this instance will continue to supervise the subordinate until the end of the program. The success of this type of program depends on the cooperation of the participants and their devotion to the program. It is absolutely essential that the coach be available both physically and intellectually to the trainee as the necessary atmosphere should be one of trust and truthfulness. The trainee should feel free to discuss his/her progress with the trainer, giving the trainer major control over the atmosphere of development. Coaching will be most successful if the coach provides a good model with whom the trainee can identify and if the coach provides adequate feedback to the trainee.

Management by Objectives

Management by objectives is a program where both the subordinate and the supervisor jointly identify the goals of the individual, and together, through feedback, monitor the success of these goals. The goals must be specific and clearly understood by both the subordinate and the superior. Also, the subordinate is given input into his/her own goals to give him/her more committment to the goals and to allow for his/her own strengths and weaknesses to be accounted for. Individual motivation and enthusiasm should be higher because the subordinate is more knowledgeable about what must be done in order for him/her to achieve desired rewards.

Although management by objectives is a very successful program, it is important that everyone in the organization be dedicated to its success. In its implementation, it is important that people are educated as to the why's and how's of the program. This training should include everyone who will be involved with management by objectives, especially the trainers and supervisors who will direct the program.

Management by objectives is basically a supportive program between superior and subordinate. There must be support, guidance and trust between the individuals or the success of the program will not be achieved. The emphasis is on problem solving and planning rather than passing judgement or blame for some past action. The system must be very flexible to change with new conditions or changes in goals due to feedback.

Management by objectives is a method where both the individual's goals and the goals of the organization can be met. Through the system of review and control the individuals can develop a team, where they will be encouraged to search together for opportunities to achieve results for everyone's benefit.

Audio/Visual Aids

Audio/visual aids can be very effective to the trainer in that these tools offer the lecturer a weapon to produce a greater impact on the senses of the trainee. In the communication process, audio/visual aids can help the trainee grasp a message and understand it. In order to use these tools effectively, the trainer must spend the time researching the material and become familiar with how to operate the tool and how to apply the material to achieve the optimal effectiveness.

In choosing the equipment to use, the trainer has many alternatives. However, it is essential that he/she keep several things in mind when deciding on the method. When using slides or any other visual medium it is important not to hit the viewer with too much information at once. Visibility and sound should be clear in order to effectively communicate the message.

Case Study

Case study as an aid to management development was initiated by the Harvard Business School. It is based on the belief that learning can best be attained through the study and discussion of situations or concrete events taken from real llife. These cases are presented in a written form to the individuals under study and they are requested to come up with ideas and possible solutions to the problem. The cases are designed to promote the trainees to think about the factors involved. In most cases, there are no absolute answers; the trainees are encouraged to be flexible and to explore all possible solutions to the existing problem.

By working with others on these cases, the trainees have a chance to exchange ideas and develop a team feeling to achieve a desired solution. It may also be argued that learning is successful in these cases because the best way to learn is to get involved in the problem and to deal with it as if it were fact. Trainees have a chance to exercise their problem-solving techniques in a group situation and may learn a great deal from the group dynamics and interaction.

Many types of cases can be used to train employees. The background case is designed to make the trainee aware of all the factors that are involved in making a decision. The complex case is designed to challenge the trainee to diagnose the underlying issues in a case, and the decision case goes even further, requiring the trainee to provide a final analysis, including a solution to the problem. Despite the depth of the case, it seems very successful in promoting planned learning and gives the trainee the opportunity to use his/her powers of perception and judgement.

Simulation

Simulations are very much like the case method, except that in simulations the cases are treated as a real-life situation. Trainees are placed in situations and are asked to deal with the problems around them—they are instructed to be themselves, and not to act. The decisions that the trainees make will have a real effect on the simulation. The simulation is followed by a critique of what went on during the exercise.

One of the most used forms of simulation is called the in-basket simulation. This is a pen and pencil exercise where the trainee is required to solve a series of problems with memos, letters and notes. The information and the time surrounding these decisions are limited. This type of exercise requires trainees to take a very active role in the program and critiques their methods of responding to the problems.

Another type of simulation that is used frequently is the business game. These range from simple non-computer exercises, which require a few days to play, to complex computer simulations, which may take weeks or months to play. Most of these games simulate a business environment with several companies competing in a common market. Decisions that must be made vary in all areas such as marketing, production, research, development and finance. The results of the decisions are computed as soon as possible, and profit-and loss-statements give the results as opposed to the competition's.

Simulations are designed to make the trainees experiment with different approaches to problem solving. These risks are allowed because the trainees do not have to face the consequences that may exist in real-life circumstances. They allow managers a chance to develop their problem-solving skills by looking both at short-term and long-term problems.

Business games may also have their shortcomings if trainees neglect to look at the exercise as a learning experience and instead try to beat the computer by devising strategies to win the game. Players of the game must then try to keep their purpose in mind so they might be able to reap the benefits of learning from the exercise.

Sources and types of **External Training** include:

1. Lecture
2. Role playing
3. Sensitivity training
4. Seminars and conferences
5. Customized workshops
6. Tapes, books and videos.

External job training is usually supplementary to on-the-job training because it is not as easily related to work tasks. This training has its advantage in the fact that trainees can give their full attention to the organized training and therefore can benefit more from external training. It allows the trainees to get away from the pressures of the job and work in an area where they would think more objectively. It provides education and new ideas which can challenge the trainee to be more motivated to self-development. Disadvantages of external training are the time and cost of the training as well as the difficulty encountered in attempting to make the training valid to the job being done.

Lecture

The lecture is still the standard form of transmitting information to a large group of people at the same time. It is very economical, although the effect on learning may be very limited. Because lectures consist of one-way communication, there is little opportunity for an exchange of ideas between the trainer and the trainees. Messages may get crossed or the meanings misunderstood and there often is little opportunity to clarify these problems. In order for a lecture to be successful, the lecturer should try to allow an exchange between himself and his trainees and he should try to make the information interesting and motivating to his listeners. Since this is very difficult, the lecture should be used with an awareness of its limitations.

Role Playing

Role playing can often be used very successfully when dealing with the case study. This would give the individuals the opportunity to play out the part they were studying. Role playing is successful in that it allows the actors to become more aware of the positions and feelings of the people they are playing. It is an effective technique for promoting attitude change, especially where conflict may exist. Although role playing may be used for a variety of different reasons, the most effective method here would be to focus on the interpersonal skills of managers in training.

Role playing has its disadvantages in that many people do not take the technique seriously and may overplay the situation. Immediate feedback is required, keeping in mind that the approval or disapproval should not be given for the acting performed but for the feeling or insight that was gained into the problem.

Sensitivity Training

The main focus of sensitivity training is on the development of individuals or groups in human relations training. This usually includes methods of unstructured group learning, individual feedback, and information sessions. Individuals are usually brought together for an extended period of time, in groups of approximately ten to twenty people. Participants work together to develop understanding of each other's experiences, feelings, reactions and behaviors. Part of this training can include role playing, case studies and other intergroup learning techniques. The basic assumption of this kind of training is that people learn best by self-discovery.

Individuals may undertake a program such as this to improve their own interpersonal skills, or groups may choose to undertake this method to improve such factors as cohesion, power, and group maturity so they can work better to achieve their common goals. These situations also give groups experience at problem solving.

Seminars and Conventions

Tying into an existing seminar or convention can provide a cost-effective method of presenting new ideas to your staff. There are a number of large, private training firms that travel across Canada and the United States offering seminars on a variety of topics, open to the general public. These seminars are normally three six hours in duration, ranging in cost from $125 to $695 per day. The size of audiences range from 20 to 6,000 people. Presenters can be consultants, university professors or the likes of Ken Blanchard or Tom Peters. Due to the nature of this type of training, there is normally a high entertainment factor and a lower education factor. It is difficult to present specific industry information to the widely diversified audiences.

Customized Workshops

Although generally more expensive than seminars and conventions, workshops can provide an excellent opportunity to offer meaningful training geared towards the organization's specific needs. Workshops work best with groups of 25 people or less. Such small groups allow for a positive ebb and flow of information between the facilitator and the audience.

Tapes, Books and Videos

A great source of training ideas can come from buying or renting training tapes, books or videos. Some of the places where one can rent this information are: public libraries, franchisors, universities, Boards of Trade, and Chambers of Commerce. Several places where this information may be purchased are: book stores and mail order catalogues.

Training Room Set-up

In order for your training efforts to have the maximum effectiveness, it is important to establish a positive atmosphere for learning. The training room set up can have a dramatic effect in creating this atmosphere. Here are some different set ups to consider:

- ☐ Is room size adequate?
- ☐ Ceiling height? Obstructions?
- ☐ Air conditioning? Individual controls?
- ☐ Lighting adequate? Dimmer switches?
- ☐ Location of doors: At rear of room?
- ☐ Any chandeliers to rattle or reflect light?
- ☐ Suited for visual aids to be used?
- ☐ Is room adequately soundproof?
- ☐ Location of electrical outlets?
- ☐ Are chairs comfortable, but firm? Arm rests?
- ☐ Are tables, visual aids, microphones available?
- ☐ Distance to elevators, washrooms, checkroom, phones.
- ☐ Is sound system adequate?
- ☐ Stage, platform, risers available?
- ☐ Can coffee be served in nearby room or foyer?
- ☐ Are window drapes "light proof"?
- ☐ Other functions scheduled in area?

Small Meeting Set-ups

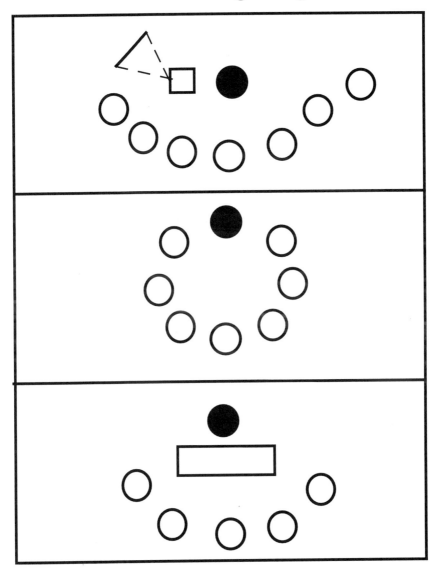

Boardroom Arrangement

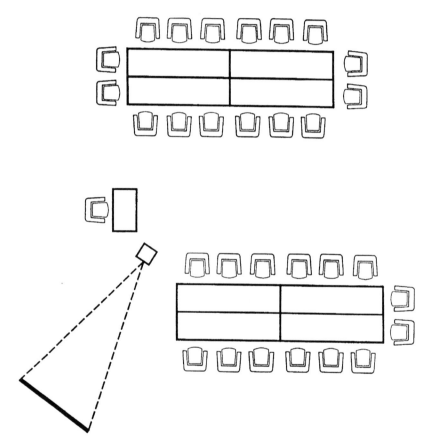

Hollow Square Arrangement

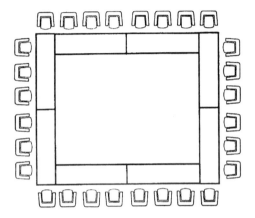

Oval Arrangement

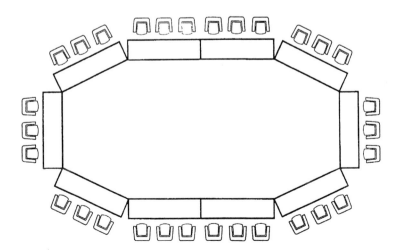

U-Shape Arrangement

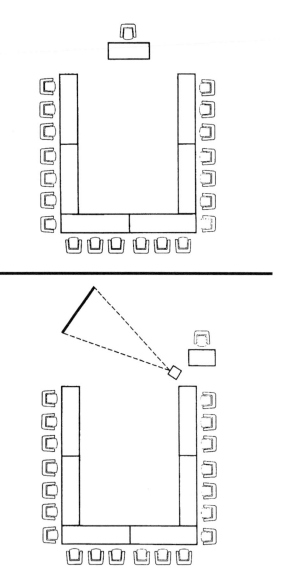

Classroom Arrangement

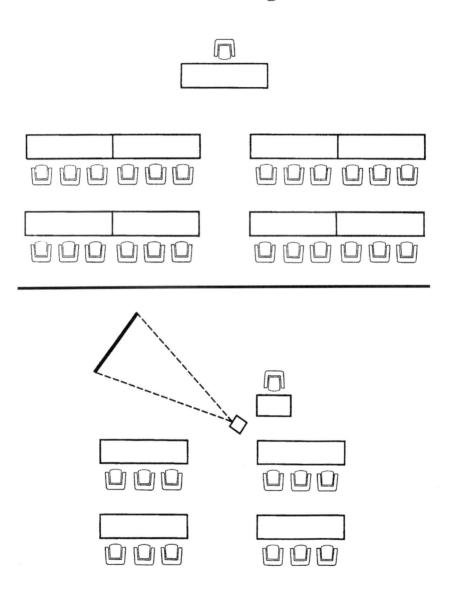

Meeting Room Graph

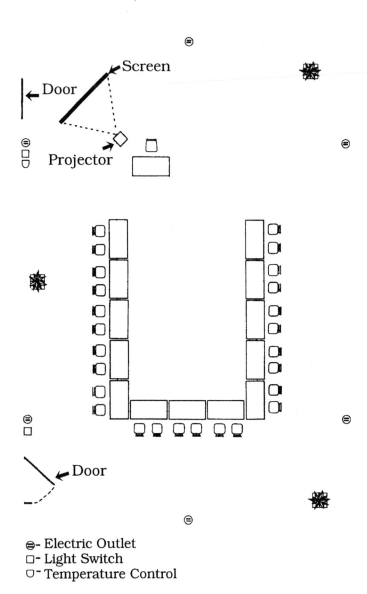

⊖ - Electric Outlet
□ - Light Switch
∪ - Temperature Control

Why Hire An Outside Trainer/Consultant?

Most managers would probably agree that at some point in time, a program needs stimulus: a breath of fresh air to promote its growth. Managers must ask themselves hard questions as they determine their suitability as trainers of their own personnel. There are issues of ability to communicate effectively, levels of current responsibility, stress factors, a manager's areas of expertise, and availability of funds to pay external trainers to be considered. If, after all questions have been addressed, external trainer services are still a possibility, there are a great many advantages to be incurred.

Trainers, when carefully selected, can bring a level of expertise not previously experienced to staff development needs. Benefits may also be derived from staff's opportunity to see themselves from the viewpoint of an outsider. This is both a frightening and exhilarating process. Managers can help to prepare staff for this experience by facilitating the outlook that a chance has arisen to identify strengths and weaknesses. If staff become defensive about what is learned, less learning and positive output is likely.

An experienced external trainer may view problems and needs from a more objective viewpoint than staff or management. At times, the investments of time and energy that go into the running of day-to-day operations of the business can prevent seeing situations and individuals in the clearest way. A fresh perspective, if one is open to it, can do wonders toward rejuvenating lagging enthusiasm. Managers, too, must refrain from being defensive when suggestions for improvement are made.

External trainers/consultants make the best staff trainers when:
- present staff lack the appropriate expertise to meet development needs
- the manager and other administrative staff are already overloaded with responsibility and cannot undertake additional tasks
- staff stress levels are high, morale is low, and revitalization is sought
- personnel communications and interaction problems exists
- a major corporate change occurs
- there is a clear need for leadership in some area that no staff member has been able to assume.

- a personnel problem has been ongoing and unresolved to date
- an unfamiliar approach or technique must be presented
- new directions or fresh perspectives are sought
- manager is not the appropriate person to respond to a staff development need

(See Appendix V for lists of associations, companies, products and topics)

Suggested Trainer Qualifications

1. Education: an advanced degree in areas of training
2. Experience: Minimum of five years practical experience
3. Philosophy: Compatible with that of the organization
4. Publications/research: Directly related to the subject matter
5. Training Experience: Minimum of three years, with a proven track record of success plus several client references
6. Personal Characteristics: Professional manner and appearance; positive and assertive in interactions with others; excellent communications skills.

(See Appendix II: Detailed Trainer Evaluation)

The Consultative Learning Process

If external trainers are to be utilized for in-house training or other staff development activities, a manager must devote some time to singling out that person or persons who are best suited to the task at hand. This can be a time consuming procedure, but it need not be complicated. The screening process suggested for selecting an external trainer is as follows:

1. The manager should know what the staff training needs are. Admittedly, there are times when assistance is required with this, but no outside person is ever aware in the way the manager/owner can be of the groups dynamics, personalities, and other factors at work. As much as it is possible, a narrowing-down process should be undertaken before seeking outside assistance.
2. Recommendations for trainers should be sought. Good sources of referrals are full time professional speakers/trainers, local colleges and universities, businesses, health care, and education programs. If colleagues have utilized consultant services, their suggestions may be the most reliable.

3. Request detailed proposals for staff development from a small, select group of trainers. Review these carefully, considering the qualifications of each, feasibility of training plans, their correlation to staff development goals, and fees charged.
4. Personally interview the two or three persons who seem to have the skills and ideas that are needed. Assess their essential personal characteristics at this time, and solicit their answers to several key questions related to their potential roles as trainers.
5. If possible, discuss the choices with your staff, and request their input. Remember, however, that the final decision rests with the manager/owner.
6. Make the decision about which trainer best meets human and organizational needs and notify that individual. Be certain to notify in writing those not selected and thank them for time and interest in providing their services.

Please note that there are circumstances under which all of the steps in the trainer selection process may not be necessary. For example: managers may have many opportunities to interact with experts in the field, attend conference workshop sessions, or hear lectures. The manager can gauge the trainer's personal charcteristics, speaking ability, expertise, and audience impact of the presenter. Additional information can always be obtained from an interview.

Briefing The Trainer

The final step in the process of retaining an external trainer is providing an in-depth briefing of the objectives to be realized and any barriers to them. The chances for trainers to be effective are reduced when information about the unique circumstances and persons to be involved is withheld.

Briefing a trainer should be a collaborative event. During this time, manager and trainer share information, describe personal needs and identify roles to be played that will facilitate the success of their efforts.

Trainer Fees

Although the selection of an external trainer should be based primarily upon an individual trainer's expertise and other skills criteria, fees charged can be a serious consideration for the manager/owner. Since many small and medium-sized businesses do not have large budgets for staff training and development, available funds must be carefully invested.

How does a manager determine what amount is reasonable payment for training fees? Since training fees can vary greatly, it may be useful for a manager to take steps to assure that the fee requested is in keeping with the service provided. The first of these steps is to survey fellow managers regarding the fees they have paid for outside training services. This can also be an excellent way of identifing the trainer with appropriate expertise.

Secondly, I suggest obtaining a written agreement with services to be provided clearly stated, along with the cost of services. This provides legal protection for both parties. Additionally, it is recommended that the degree of experience of the trainer should be a factor in the fee paid. An individual with considerable consultation background would be justified in charging a higher fee than someone with less experience.

Lastly, I would recommend that unless a manager has been referred to a trainer by a highly respected colleague, he or she should request references from previous clients.

Adult Learning

When selecting people, we examine their knowledge, skills and attitude. We have to consider all three components as they relate to these two key questions.

1. Can this person do this job? (Does he/she have the skills and knowledge?)
2. Will he/she consistently do a good job over a long period of time? (What is his/her attitude?)

Even if someone possesses the right combination of the three traits, no one is perfect and some additional training will be required in the future. It is important to differentiate among these terms as they relate to adult learning and training.

Skill: Refers to the trainee's ability to do things. Skills can be; assembling, collating, problem solving, decision making, etc..

Attitude: Refers to beliefs, feelings, values, opinions, desires, expectations, temperaments, etc,—the factors relating to the trainee's personality and the way the individual has been conditioned by parents, teachers, friends, former employers, and the environment (both off and on the job).

Knowledge: Refers to facts, concepts, principles, rules, procedures and information or "subject matter" that the trainee needs to know.

Triangle of Success in Hiring and Training

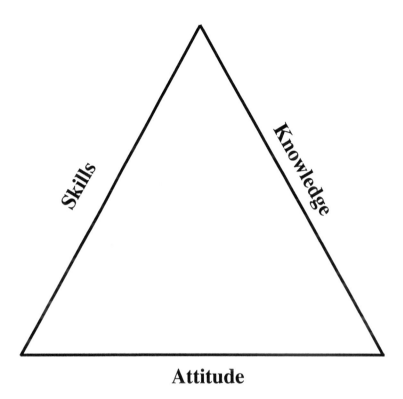

If staff were all alike, training would be a simple task. Everyone would learn in the same way and at the same rate. However, there are no two individuals alike. Employees differ from one another in their experiences, looks, likes and dislikes, understanding, and rate of learning.

The purpose of this section is to present some very basic ideas and principles about the way people learn. An understanding of why and how people learn will help you to be a better trainer.

Learning is a lifelong, continuing process of acquiring knowledge, attitudes and skills. When individuals want to learn, and have taken the steps necessary to apply what they have learned, learning, has taken place.

The experience of learning leads to changes within the individual. Learning, then, can be defined as "a change in an employee's behavior resulting from experience."

What Change do You Want in Your Trainee's Behaviour?

To be effective, training must address all three parts of human behaviour—what the trainee knows (knowledge), how the trainee feels (attitude), and what skills the trainee has. Every learning situation should have these three elements.

In helping individuals learn, you must identify the changes that you want to occur in the learner. You have to know exactly what the objectives for learning are.

Ask yourself the following questions:

1. What specific knowledge or understanding do you want to teach?
2. What new skills do you want the trainee to learn?
3. What new attitudes and values do you want the trainee to have?

For example, knowing the procedures for effective interviewing (knowledge) is different from being able to demonstrate effective interviewing techniques (a skill), both of which differ from wanting to use them on the job (attitude).

Structure the training-learning process to help learners achieve the required results.

Example: Suppose we were training a bricklayer. Most people would think of bricklaying as a skill, requiring much more practice than knowledge or attitude. However, if we were to analyze the behavior of a competent bricklayer, we would find that all three components of our "training triangle" had been highly developed. Our analysis might look something like the table on the following page.

Knowledge	Attitude	Skill
• Correct proportions of sand, mortar, lime to meet different conditions of the brick and the weather. • Procedure for testing sand for its organic content (and, thus, its acceptability). • Patterns of brick: English, Flemish, common bond, use of header courses. • Use of weep holes, expansion joint, tie-rods, reinforcing bars. • Procedures for executing jambs, lintels, corbels, vaults and arches, gables, parapets buttresses, freeform curves.	• Pride in work, high degree of craftsmanship and professionalism. • Appreciation of the appearance of well-laid brick. • Neatness in maintaining work area, cleaning tools, putting materials away at end of the day. • Recognition of the importance of following safety rules and practices, even when they take longer. • Desire to work in cost-effective manner, working as fast as possible without sacrificing quality.	• Cutting brick with one blow of mason's hammer or cold chisel. • Mixing mortar to workable consistency not too stiff, not too runny. • Taking mortar from mortarboard to trowel to brick without spilling or discoloring the surface of the wall. • Techniques for finishing joints—flush, raked, raised. • Use of the level and plumb line so wall is level and plumb. • Use of trowel in "buttering" the ends of bricks with just enough mortar.

Knowledge, Attitude, Skill Exercise

Suppose you have just been promoted and you have only one week to train your replacement. List the most important knowledge, attitudes, and skills of your present job that you would want to develop in your replacement.

Knowledge	Attitude	Skill

4 Levels of Learning

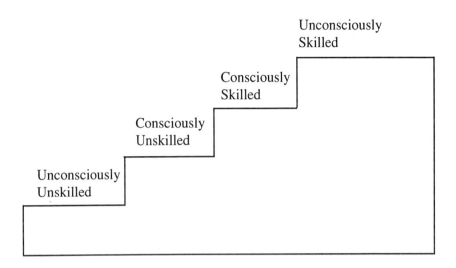

Trainers must realize there are different levels of learning.

1. The first level of learning is called unconsciously unskilled; this is when the trainees do not possess the desired skills nor are they aware that they do not possess them.
2. The second level of learning is one of awareness. This is when the individual becomes consciously aware that he/she is unskilled.
3. The third level of learning can be an awkward phase, where the employee has learned a new skill and is conscious of it. Employees at this stage often suffer from a "mightier than thou" complex.
4. When an employee has mastered a skill to the point where it is second nature, we say that he/she is unconsciously skilled. The example here would be the hockey goalie who deflects a stray rock that has been hurled at him by a passing car.

There are three basic ways of learning:

1. Trial and error
2. Imitation
3. Structured learning

Trial-and-error learning occurs when individuals are left to develop their own solutions to problems. Trainees must be motivated to learn by this method. The trial-and-error process is usually not time-efficient but does produce permanent learning.

- effective application: rolling a coin.
- ineffective application: landing a 747 jet.

Learning will take place more quickly if the trainee has a model to imitate. By using "experts" as role models, special techniques or tricks of the trade can be learned quickly. However, if underlying principles of behavior cannot be seen, trainees will learn only superficial aspects of the skill.

- effective application: printing the alphabet.
- ineffective application: granting a loan.

Structured learning refers to any form of learning controlled or guided by a trainer or training materials. This control may be informal (coaching) or very formal (self instructional texts). In general, this method is good for complex tasks but may not be useful for simple learning or attitude change.

- effective application: landing a 747 jet.
- ineffective application: changing a light bulb.

Laws of Learning

Although psychologists and educators have been studying learning seriously since the turn of the century, only a few "laws of learning" have been discovered or proven. Knowledge of these laws may guide you in changing behavior in others.

The Law of . . .

Effect

This law states that people learn best in pleasant physical and psychological surroundings. People are more likely to accept and repeat those activities and responses that are pleasant and satisfying to them.

You can improve your training by providing your trainees with the opportunity to succeed early in their training and by giving appropriate rewards for trainee efforts. You should also provide a friendly and comfortable atmosphere for your training sessions.

Exercise

This law states that people learn best by doing. The old saying that "PRACTICE MAKES PERFECT" is also part of this law. Each time a task is accomplished, it helps to fix the method. Repetition strengthens the learning and helps to retain the skill just as disuse weakens the skill. Learning to ride a bicycle is an example of the law of exercise. You learn to ride a bike by **riding** the bike; trying over and over again until you can master the activity.

You can improve your training by involving your trainees in learning and by giving them plenty of opportunities to practice new tasks and skills.

Readiness

This law states that adults learn best when they feel there is a need— when it is to their benefit to learn. When adults feel the need to learn, the motivation is already there and your task becomes that much easier.

You can improve your training by showing trainees why the learning is important and how it relates to their job situation. Let your trainees know what benefits they will gain from the training.

Association

This law states that every new fact, idea or concept is best learned if you can relate it to already known information. Learning can be compared to children's building blocks where new blocks are added to the existing set; you add each new bit of information to your existing body of information.

You can improve your training by relating new information to earlier experiences or knowledge. Your task as a trainer is to guide your trainees from "where they are" to "where you want them to be." Build from the simple to the complex.

Six Truths of Learning

The following is a summary of generally accepted truths derived from the laws of learning. They can help you to better understand how people learn.

1. People learn at different rates;

    Trainees differ in background, motivation, work habits and learning ability. Trainers must be ready to adjust to these individual differences. Be prepared to step in with a word of encouragement when a trainee has a bad day or when he/she has trouble coping with difficult material.

2. People learn better when you appeal to all their senses;

   Trainees will remember better if they "see" as well as "hear" what is being taught. Bring your material alive with examples, illustrations and demonstrations. A vivid, exciting learning experience is more likely to be remembered than a routine or boring one.

3. People need to know when they have done a good job;

   Positive reinforcement provides the incentive to learn. People accept and repeat those activities that are pleasant and satisfying. A good trainer can make sure every trainee experiences some satisfaction in learning.

4. People learn better by looking at the "big picture" first;

   Your training will be more effective when you use the whole-part-whole approach. Start your training sessions by looking at the "big picture" or the entire job first. Then break down the job into its smaller tasks and show how each piece fits into the puzzle. Individual parts of a job should be explained in detail only after your trainees understand the overall job.

5. People learn better if they concentrate on one learning task at a time;

   Too much information will produce anxiety in your trainees. Information is better recalled when seven or less points are used.

6. People must be given a chance to actually experience the things they have been learning;

   Your training will be more effective when your trainees can practice their new skills on the job. For example, a Loans Officer will learn how to grant a loan much faster by actually doing it than by reading about it.

   Adults need to be motivated in order to learn. The problem that most trainers face is in knowing what motivates trainees. To ensure your trainees are motivated, you must relate the contents of your training program to one or more of your trainee's needs.

Individuals have two types of needs. Job needs relate to their job situation. People are usually aware of them and willing to discuss them. Personal needs are often unconscious.

This list gives you examples of both types of needs.

JOB NEEDS	PERSONAL NEEDS
Doing a good job	A sense of accomplishment
Adequate salary	An opportunity to grow
Promotions	A feeling of pride
Salary increase	Recognition for ability and efforts
Easier work	A voice in decisions that affect me
Lack of confusion on the job	Authority
Titles commensurate with responsibility	Honest praise
	Time to socialize
Fair treatment	Being in the know
Equal opportunities	Being comfortable in associations and tasks
Good working conditions	
Interesting work	Security
Security	Friendship and approval
Recognition	Lack of worry
Feeling of belonging	Lack of risks
	Lack of embarrassment
	Knowledge of the environment

Identify the needs of your trainees and propel them into action by matching elements of your training to one or more of their needs. By doing so, the trainee becomes emotionally involved (motivated) towards the training. Once this connection occurs the probability of success increases tenfold.

15 Characteristics of a Good Trainer

Friendly	—creates a warm and comfortable atmosphere.
	—speaks in a friendly tone.
Patient	—adjusts to task difficulties.
	—makes sure everyone understands what is expected.
	—controls anger.
Fair	—adjusts to individual trainee differences.
	—avoids favoritism.

Enthusiastic	—is motivated. —demonstrates a positive attitude to training. —inspires enthusiasm for training in others.
Humorous	—shows a natural humour that is part of the thought, and not forced. —creates a positive feeling in the work group. —stimulates and arouses learning.
Empathetic	—understands people's feelings and attitudes. —acts approvingly and supportively of people.
Creative	—provides a variety of different approaches to training sessions. —highlights training with appropriate and varied examples.
Honest	—admits to being wrong. —tells it "like it is," not what it should be like.
Open Minded	—gives and takes constructive criticism. —is ready and willing to learn.
Cooperative	—shares information and gives reasons for directions. —shares own experiences as well as others.
Confident:	—is at ease and in control. —shows confidence in others.
Respectful of people	—likes and trusts people. —acknowledges people's names. —focuses on participant's behavior and not on personality or attitude only. —enjoys the respect of trainees.
Interested	—wants to teach people to work as a group. —is available before, during and after work hours.
Observant	—is alert and in control. —is quick to respond and set things right. —watches for feelings, i.e.: frustration, boredom.
A good listener	—listens for feelings, i.e.: anger, sadness, confusion. —listens for what is meant, not said. —concentrates and does not interrupt.

Training Evaluation Exercise

1. Evaluate your effectiveness as a trainer, by using the Trainer Evaluation Sheet on the next page.
2. Use copies of this Trainer Evaluation Sheet as a checklist in each of your future training efforts.

Use these evaluations to identify your weak areas. Work on improving one area at a time. You will benefit only if you are honest in your evaluations.

Trainer Evaluation Sheet

Use this form to evaluate yourself as a trainer.
How effective are you in:

	Very Good	Good	Fair	Poor
1. Selecting the appropriate location for training				
2. Scheduling training to minimize distractions and interruptions				
3. Having all needed materials (forms, tools, checklists) on hand				
4. Organizing the teaching into the most logical sequence				
5. Knowing the subject matter				
6. Managing the time well				
7. Setting trainee at ease right at the start				
8. Stating objectives in terms meaningful to the trainee				
9. Finding out learner's knowledge, skills, and attitudes				
10. Explaining the who, what, when, where and why of training and the job				
11. Explaining and demonstrating, simultaneously when possible				
12. Using language, terms, and examples that the trainee understands				

13. Explaining why things are done as they are			
14. Having trainee perform and explain why the task is done that way			
15. Asking questions that get meaningful responses from the trainee			
16. Frequently giving feedback that is specific and immediate			
17. Correcting mistakes constructively			
18. Giving positive reinforcement where appropriate			
19. Keeping the trainee actively participating and performing			
20. Serving as coach and not as "expert" dispensing information			
21. Putting trainee on the job with close observation			
22. Introducing other workers as sources of help on the job			
23. Tapering off the instruction			
24. Continuing evaluation and follow-up with normal supervision			

You can determine from this questionnaire what areas you are strong in and what areas need work.

Conclusion

Although there are many types of training that can be taken for employee improvement, there are some factors that must be remembered. First of all, individual differences must be remembered and each success must depend on the trainee's motivation to learn the desired information. Motivation in certain training activities is likely to depend on how actively the trainee engaged in the training process. Feedback is also very important to reinforce the trainee's program and to answer any questions which may not have come up during the training process. Training programs should be evaluated to make sure they are achieving the desired results. They must remain flexible to be able to meet changing demands in the work environment and to positively contribute toward keeping staff productive and happy.

Chapter Three

MOTIVATING STAFF: FACT OR FICTION

I sincerely believe that when it comes to finding and keeping great staff that one of the key elements is attitude. If you look at the diagram on page 71 it says "Triangle of Success in Hiring and Training." This particular triangle has "Skills" on one side, "Knowledge" on the other side, and "Attitude" on the bottom. "Skills" are the individuals' previous experiences, their ability to do the job. That's also true with knowledge. "Knowledge" is the formal education received, the courses taken, and the books read. Now when you bring these two areas together—"Skills" and "Knowledge," basically you're asking, "Can the person physically do the job?"

Unfortunately, in the past, when it comes to hiring staff, most people have stopped at just that. We have to go much further. I think you have to look at the second issue: attitude. The second thing we have to consider is "Can the person do the job well, and will the person do the job well over the long haul?" This is an attitude issue. One thing I often say in my seminars—when it comes to hiring and keeping staff—is that attitude is 85 per cent of one's success.

Attitude is also one's level of motivation. Now, a lot of managers feel that it's their responsibility to motivate staff. I would actually disagree with that. In fact, I'm of the opinion that it's absolutely impossible to motivate another human being. However, I do believe that the person can be enticed to make changes him/herself. But when push comes to shove, I think the onus has to be on the individual to make the decision to change, and to motivate himself/herself.

I'll give you an example. We often hear the maxim, "We can take a horse to water, but we can't make him drink." In fact, we can even walk the horse over to the water and say "Hey, horse, look outside, isn't that a hot day? Don't you feel hot? Aren't you thirsty? Look at that beautiful creek. Doesn't that water look great? Of course it does. Here, let me show you how good it is," and get down and actually drink the water.

Now even after doing all that, if the horse decides that he's not going to drink, *he's not going to drink.* There's nothing you can do to force him to drink. And I think adults are very similar. What you can do, and you're supposed to do, in my estimation, as managers and supervisors and business owners, is to create an environment that makes it easier for the employee to make the right decisions. In other words, to create a motivating environment. I think that if you also have the expectation that it's up to us to change and motivate our staff, then I think you're going to set yourselves up for some failure and some disappointments.

Now the next diagram below, called "Motivation and Work Performance," is an attempt to explain what the average employee requires in

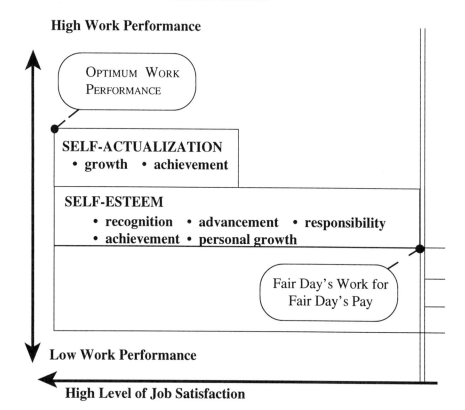

order to become motivated. I've looked at the work of two noted psychologists in the area, Hertzberg and Maslow. Both studied these issues quite extensively.

I looked at what they were saying and from there I have made my own interpretations and blended their work together and created this new model. I really believe that Hertzberg and Maslow were saying essentially the same thing using different examples and different terms.

Going through the model, on the right side, there is something that looks like a stepping stone. It starts off at the bottom with very basic needs or physiological needs. Maslow called his theory "The Hierarchy of Needs." His premise was very simple: everyone starts out wanting and being motivated to acquire very basic or physiological needs. Some of these needs are **personal safety, food, clothing, shelter**.

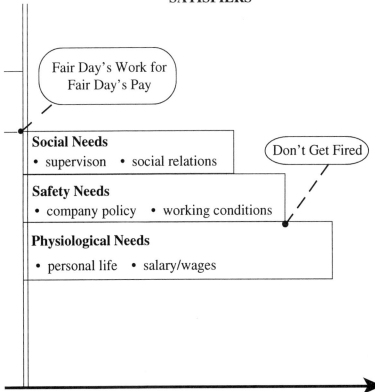

How it worked was, if you wanted somebody to dig a ditch, and the person you wanted to dig the ditch was very hungry and didn't have any food, you came along and offered that person a hamburger or steak or whatever and said, "Listen, if you dig this ditch, I'm going to give you some food." Because you can provide them with something to satisfy that very basic need, that <u>food</u> becomes motivation for the individual. It will actually motivate them to want to do the work.

Now, let's assume you came across somebody else. But this other person has a full stomach. Their fridge and their pantry is absolutely full of food. This person now has their very basic needs fulfilled and somewhat saturated. Offering them more food will probably not be motivating for them. So they're not likely to dig the ditch for you, if that's the only incentive you can offer.

But Maslow said once we have our basic needs met, we're now triggered or motivated to move on to higher-level needs. So, the next level up is something called "Safety Needs." Being in a safe environment and being out of harm's way, does not mean working with dangerous equipment. Once this level has been met, then the next level in the hierarchy is called "Social Needs."

Maslow believed that humans were very social people, and would require over the long haul all sorts of loving, nurturing supportive relationships. Now, once these three basic levels have been met, the next step or the next phase in the Hierarchy of Needs is something called "Self-Esteem."

Now I'll paint a very simple definition of self-esteem. It's how much you like or love yourself. I'm not talking about someone who's very conceited, but someone who can simply look at him/herself and say, "Hey, sure I have some weaknesses, but I also have some strengths." These people can acknowledge their own good and be comfortable with themselves. And that's a very important measure. I think that any time you can offer somebody some way or some conditions that will satisfy his/her need for a high level of self-esteem, that becomes very motivational.

Lastly, Maslow said the highest level within the Hierarchy of Needs is something called "Self-Actualization." In my way of thinking, self-actualization is simply when you're walking down the road of life and you're totally satisfied and you have a (wonderful) balance in every area of your life. That's being totally self-actualized.

Now, the other gentleman, Hertzberg, viewed motivation in the individual as it related to work he/she did. What he did was divide the model down the center. He broke it down into two sides. On one side, he had something called "Satisfiers." And on the other side he had the "Motivators."

Now another word to put beside "Satisfiers" is "Hygiene Factors." Now why are they called "Hygiene Factors?" Well, looking back to when you were young children, back in school, remember the public health nurse who made periodic visits? What did she normally say? She would say in order to maintain good personal hygiene, we have to brush our teeth, comb our hair, wash our face . . . so on and so forth.

Let me ask you a question. If you brush your teeth on a regular basis three times a day, that's great. But if you start brushing your teeth maybe 20, 30, 40 times a day, will you become healthier? I would suggest that not only would you not become healthier, but you may even become ill by actually doing some damage to your gums. Now, on the flip side, if one day you just simply stop brushing your teeth, you also could become ill because of the onset of cavities and germs and so on and so forth. So why is it called "Hygiene Factors?" Basically, the whole idea is if you don't supply these core needs to the employee over the long haul, then the employee in a sense will become "sick."

These are all the things that Maslow mentioned in the first three basic levels. One, having adequate wage and salary, means having enough money to live and having enough time away from the job to have some sort of decent personal life. Two, to have pro-active and safe working conditions, and to have a humane company policy. Three, having the opportunity to interact with supportive co-workers and subordinates as well as supervisors.

These three areas put together, if given in abundance, don't actually make for a healthy employee. Nor does it make a peak performer. However, according to Hertzberg, if we remove any one of these core elements over a long period of time, even the most satisfied, most highly motivated employees will start to drop off. Their level of productivity and motivation will drop right down to the point where they're only going to give you enough performance so they don't get fired.

Now, if you provide your employees with these three conditions, and you only meet these three conditions and don't give anything above, then what you can expect to get out of these people—at the very most—is only a fair day's work for a fair day's pay. If you're like me and you require absolute peak performers working for your organization, then you will have to pay a little bit more, and I'm not necessarily talking about salary.

Now what's the price you have to pay for peak performers? Let's look at the other side of the diagram. You have to provide true motivators. You have to provide the pre-conditions within the work environment to excite the employees so that they become self-motivated. What are these five motivators?

Number One: **A sense of Responsibility.** Staff need to feel that their level of responsibility will actually grow over a period of time within the job.

Number Two: **Advancement.** There has to exist an opportunity for advancement within the organization.

Number Three: **Recognition.** Everyone seeks feedback. One of the problems, of course, is that sometimes the only feedback given from management is when something is done wrong. One of the cautions that I give management is not to get involved in what I call "Peek-a-boo management." Peek-a-boo management is when you hide around a corner and peer around with one eye and just wait 'til somebody messes up so you can say, "Peek-a-boo, gotcha. Now I'm going to get you."

There's a problem with that sort of mindset. I sincerely believe that if an employee is doing something wrong, the (performer's) problem must be corrected immediately, so it doesn't become a habit. However, I believe in looking at this from the opposite perspective. I got this idea from Ken Blanchard's wonderful book, *The One-Minute Manager*. Basically, Blanchard says, "Catch them doing something *right*. Management should be deliberately catching staff doing something right." Not only saying, "Have you done something right? "But," let me tell you what you did right, what you liked about it, and the positive effect it has on the organization."

Now if you take the time to do this, first of all the employees will love the positive feedback. They're going to feel very good about the process. It's going to add to the rapport and the relationship between you and your employees. And, perhaps even more importantly, they're going to continue the positive behaviour. And this is very important.

After Recognition, the fourth motivator is **Achievement.** The staff needs the opportunity to achieve success in the workplace.

And lastly, an opportunity for **Personal Growth** is the fifth motivator. One way could be in the form of promotions. But it could be giving out more responsibilities and more senior tasks.

Before I go much further in my discussion about staff motivation, I think it would be appropriate to take the time to dispell 10 Motivational Myths.

Motivational Myth Number 1: Cash is King

The idea that money is the most important or the most powerful human motivator is perhaps the most common—and perhaps even the most dangerous—of all the Motivational Myths. In fact, one of the things I sincerely believe is that money is not a motivator in the long run. Let me explain this in more detail.

I believe if someone doesn't have enough money to pay their bills and take care of their debts, then of course money becomes a motivator. This is a very primary need within the Hierarchy of Needs, according to Maslow. Once someone has enough money to meet their basic needs, and perhaps just a little bit left over, money becomes much less of a motivator. The nature of the job, the type of people, the work hours: all these things become much more important factors in motivating the employee.

For example, have you ever known anyone—perhaps even yourself—who has been offered a different job that would have paid a lot more money than what he/she was making, but he/she decided not to choose that job because of a number of other variables? Maybe it was the kind of work that led them to this choice, where you would have to be geographically, the hours, and so on and so forth. So here's proof that money is not the prime motivator of staff.

Motivational Myth Number 2: Motivation Equals Productivity

Although there is some sort of linkage between employees that are highly motivated and those that are highly productive, there isn't a 100 percent cause-effect relationship. There could be someone who is highly motivated, really wants to do the job, is very enthusiastic, and has a wonderful attitude, but doesn't have the training. He/she doesn't have the background skills and knowledge, or the aptitude. For example, just because you want to be a brain surgeon, you really believe that you're a brain surgeon, and you've even visualized in your mind being a successful brain surgeon—if you haven't gone to medical school, and you haven't taken the time to study it and spend the years involved in preparing to become a brain surgeon, you will not have the productivity required to be a brain surgeon.

Motivational Myth Number 3:
YOU CAN MOTIVATE ANOTHER PERSON

As you probably already know, nobody can make a smoker stop smoking, an alcoholic stop drinking, or a gambler stop gambling. No manager can cause an employee to be motivated. But a manager can provide the **means** and the **atmosphere** for employees to motivate themselves.

An employee will only be **motivated** when he/she has a **need that is currently unmet**, and that's an individual need. When this need exists in this individual, the employee will naturally take steps to satisfy this need. So one of the tricks of management is to see the trends within each individual, to see which particular needs need to be fulfilled. Then, as a manager, you must determine and present to your employee a means or a strategy to satisfy this need while tying into the specific objectives of the organization, and then, monitor the results.

Motivational Myth Number 4:
HAPPY EMPLOYEES ARE PRODUCTIVE EMPLOYEES

Well, happy employees are definitely happy employees. And that's nice. But that is not enough. That's not enough if you're looking for highly productive people. When push comes to shove in business, what you are really looking for is productivity and output. And someone smiling is not enough. The best scenario, of course, is to have a highly productive employee who also happens to be happy and friendly and smiles a lot and is a very sociable individual.

Motivational Myth Number 5:
WHAT MOTIVATES ME MOTIVATES EVERYONE ELSE

Unfortunately, motivators are not universal. One employee may be absolutely delighted that you cared enough for him/her, that you remembered his/her birthday. And in doing so, he/she may improve output by several hundred per cent. Another employee, however, may sneer when he/she is awarded the Employee of the Year Award, and may actually show no improvement in productivity. Some employees simply want to do their job on a nine-to-five basis, they work at a fair, but even pace, they are neither satisfied nor dissatisfied, and they are not upwardly mobile. They do not want to take on any more responsibility.

Some other employees are like small children: they need constant prodding, supervision, and hand-holding. Their managers are always trying to think of critical ways to provide incentives that boost their productivity. Where other employees are easily motivated, any kind of response—whether positive or negative—from management is a push forward for them. Other employees are powerhouses of productivity. These people are self-motivated.

The point is that people are different. Every employee is different. Therefore, you have to make sure that you tailor some of your activities to each employee to try to meet his/her specific motivational requirements.

Motivational Myth Number 6:
DISINCENTIVES CAN BE USED TO AID IN MOTIVATION

If you can't get an employee to do the job, you can always resort to some form of punishment, can't you? You can teach them a lesson. Well, maybe you can, and it might have a short-term benefit. But behavioral psychologists have demonstrated in various studies that over time negative reinforcement is less effective as a means of changing long-term behavior than positive reinforcement. This is covered in more detail in Chapter Six, "Positive Discipline."

One of the cautions I would like to say at this point, though, is not to apply discipline in the hope that you can whip your employees into shape. I really think that it can be a detrimental process to the relationship, not to mention it can undermine the integrity of the individual, and at best, it's only a short-term fix.

Motivational Myth Number 7:
THE BOSS DOESN'T HAVE TO BE PERSONALLY MOTIVATED TO HAVE A MOTIVATED STAFF

To this I say hogwash! It's absolutely imperative that the captain of the team—the manager, the owner, the leader—has to be motivated and has to encourage staff to manage themselves. The best way to do this is through mirroring, by being the staff's role model. To best accomplish this a manager should simply live the motivational life. Then people will look up to you and mirror what you do.

Motivational Myth Number 8:
IF MY EMPLOYEES ARE MOTIVATED, I'LL EASILY BE ABLE TO SEE IT

Well, this myth is a common misconception in many management circles. Unfortunately, motivation can't be measured by some sort of "smile-o-meter." Some employees are naturally stoic. Their seemingly lacklustre demeanor is not necessarily a reflection of a lack of motivation on their part, it might just represent their personality. They don't show their enthusiasm very much. Yet when you look at the end result, they're highly productive people. They're very motivated to do what is necessary on their job.

Motivational Myth Number 9:
IT'S UP TO THE SUPERVISORS AND LINE MANAGERS TO MOTIVATE STAFF

That's simply not true. I think it's up to every single individual within the organization to be motivated, to be self-motivated. But it has to start from somewhere. Where it has to start is from the very top down, right from the CEO, the president of the organization. These individuals have to be motivated. They have to be able to exude a real energy and charisma about them. And they have to be able to sell their vision of their organization to everyone within the company.

Motivational Myth Number 10:
IF 75 PER CENT OF YOUR EMPLOYEES ARE MOTIVATED, THEN YOU'VE GOT NOTHING TO WORRY ABOUT

Well, I disagree. Even if you have a very small percentage of your staff that has a poor attitude, who are unmotivated and have the wrong kind of attitude, they can ruin the corporate culture within your organization very quickly. All you need is one "bad apple" to spoil the whole "bushel." If just one person within your department or organization has a motivational problem, that problem can easily spread to other people on the staff.

Here are some ideas on how to avoid this problem. 1) Try to intercede any sort of negative discussions that take place by helping people turn the negatives into positives. 2) Make an extra effort to provide additional incentives to the entire staff. 3) Hold frequent group meetings in which you can head off many of the negative vibes and actually deal with any real concerns that the unhappy employee may be expressing.

How do you determine what your employees really want? As I mentioned before, no two people are the same. No two of your employees are alike. Consequently, no single motivator is going to work as well with each and every one of your employees. To motivate effectively with non-monetary incentives, you need to know more about what the various motivators are. You need to know what will work with each and every one of your staff.

The reality is that the values of the 1990's and beyond are very different than the values of the workers of the 1950's and '60's. Because of high-tech information, the advances in media, and a myriad of other factors, today's workers are better educated, more independent, and less interested in following orders. They are more loyal to themselves than to the organization, and they are more concerned and vocal about meeting their own personal needs. The contemporary employee wants meaningful, challenging work, wants to spend a lot more of his/her time in leisure activities, has a very strong need for feedback and recognition, and would like to see immediate payback for the efforts put into a job.

Many of the employers that I have talked to assumed that they knew exactly what their workers wanted and believed that they were doing a good job of providing it. For example, they would point directly at the good wage and benefit packages that they provided as tangible proof that they were taking care of their employees. But many times—and I took the time to ask the same question of the employees to find out what they wanted—I found that no, the wage and salary portion of the job wasn't as significant a motivator as the manager thought, and there were other parts of the job that were much more important.

A 1969 study by the Research Center at the University of Michigan looked at the attitudes of 1,533 workers at different occupational levels. All these workers ranked "interesting work" and "the authority to get the job done" as far more important than good pay and job security. These same findings were confirmed by similar studies in both 1973 and 1978. Further, 327 school principals from Alberta, Canada, were asked to complete a questionnaire assessing their job satisfaction. Eight satisfaction factors were identified through Factor Analysis, and three were determined to contribute to the most overall job satisfaction. They were "responsibility," "autonomy," and "principal-teacher work involvement." Interestingly enough, salary and benefits did not contribute significantly to the overall job satisfaction of those taking that particular survey.

Ask yourself this: "Do you really know what your employees want?" To determine just how much your perception of what your employees want can differ from what they really want, complete **Worksheet #1**, called **"Staff Motivators,"** below. Take your time and ask your employees to complete it. The discrepancies that may arise in how you and your staff rank different aspects of employment might be very surprising to you.

Worksheet #1 Staff Motivators

Rank from **1** to **10**—10 being what you think your employees least want from their jobs—in the manager column. Circulate the list among your employees. Ask them to rank the order of importance from their perspective in the employee column.

Category	Manager	Employee
Help with personal problems	_____	_____
Interesting work	_____	_____
High wages	_____	_____
Job security	_____	_____
Personal loyalty of a supervisor	_____	_____
Tactful discipline	_____	_____
Full appreciation of work done	_____	_____
A sense of belonging	_____	_____
Pro-active working conditions	_____	_____
The opportunity for promotion in company	_____	_____

What is the quickest way for you to determine what really motivates your employees? First, ask them. Go to your employees and ask them specifically what they like most and least about their jobs. Ask them questions such as *"What are some of the things the company is doing that increases your self-esteem? What are some of the things that the company does that decreases your levels of self-esteem?"* Their answers can be the starting point in discovering what motivates each and every member of your staff.

The second thing you could do is to find out what your employees do in their spare time, both at work and at home. This will tell you more about your employees.

Thirdly, look to previous experiences within the company. What sort of tasks or experiences has the employee responded very favourably to in the past? What types of projects or assignments really created a high level of productivity? What types of assignments created apathy in the employee? And can we learn from this analysis? A more formalized method of determining what motivates your staff is to use a survey designed by Dick Berry, an Associate Professor of Management and Administrator of Management Institutes and Marketing Management program. His survey is called the **"Motiquiz III."** It's shown here as **Worksheet #2**.

Worksheet #2.

This survey contains 45 statements describing different situations. Motiquiz is an exercise to determine motivational needs. To perform the exercise, for each of the following statements check those that are **most** important in motivating you to do your best work. Select the ten most important statements. When you're done, then refer to the scoring guide at the bottom after you've made your selections.

- 629: Job security because of seniority or employment contract arrangements.
- 847: Being trusted to do my job the way I think it should be done.
- 333: Participating in a workgroup conversation.
- 311: Having adequate shelter to protect from the elements.
- 836: Having a job which allows me the time with my family.
- 151: Having an opportunity for personal growth.
- 937: Socializing with my friends.
- 743: Being considered for advancement opportunity.
- 431: Working with other people.
- 819: Having children.
- 458: Doing something meaningful with my life.
- 757: Being in a position to contribute new ideas.
- 828: Having an associate that looks out for my interests.
- 215: Not having to do exhausting work or do extra work at home.
- 421: Having steady work.
- 654: Being able to express my full potential.
- 327: Knowing that I will always have a job.

912: Having rest breaks with nourishments available.
924: Having a healthy working environment.
548: Being given a new interesting job.
256: Having the opportunity for self-improvement.
722: Having protection from physical harm.
352: Being able to learn and grow in my work.
735: Including other people in what I do.
949: Being selected for an exclusive award.
234: Being involved with work associates in social and recreational activities.
616: Being sexually satisfied.
146: Having a responsible person tell me when I've done a good job.
539: Having an active part in work-related social activities.
341: Knowing that other people respect me and my work.
132: Acceptance as a workgroup member.
225: Having insurance or other protective benefits.
444: Having others recognize the importance of my job.
853: Having a new and exciting job challenge.
113: Having enough food to eat each day.
245: Not having to be responsible to other people.
517: Having personal comfort in my working environment.
126: Knowing what is expected of me in my work.
559: Having the opportunity to express myself fully and creatively.
718: Having good air to breath.
638: Working with persons I want to associate with.
642: Having a position of authority.
523: A guaranteed income.
955: The personal satisfaction of a job well done.
414: The assurance that I will have adequate clothing to protect myself from the elements.

Scoring Instructions for the Motiquiz

To determine the results, the statements are divided into five categories intended to represent the five levels in Maslow's Hierarchy of Needs. The second digit in each statement number indicates the category. These categories are (1) Physiological; (2) Safety and Security; (3) Social Needs; (4) Self-esteem; (5) Self-actualization.

The employee's motivational needs are suggested by the numbers of selections in each category. For example, if the person had one in (1), two in (2), one in (3), four in (4), and two in (5), the percentage would be 10 percent Physiological, 20 percent Safety Needs, 10 percent Social Needs, 40 percent Self-esteem, and 20 percent for Self-actualization.

Another method of finding out what motivates the employee is to have him/her fill out the **Values Preference Chart** listed below.

Values Preference Chart

Work Interests & Aptitudes:	Low				High
	1	2	3	4	5

Physical work (fixing, building, using hands) _____

Written work (writing, reading, using words) _____

Oral work (talking, giving speeches)_____

Quantitative work (data, using numbers)_____

Visual work (watching, inspecting)_____

Interpersonal work (counselling, interviewing)_____

Creative work (inventing, designing, ideas)_____

Analytical work (doing research, solving problems)_____

Managerial work (initiating, coordinating)_____

Clerical work (keeping records)_____

Outdoor work (construction, travelling)_____

Mechanical work (repairing, fixing, tinkering)_____

	Low				High
IDENTIFYING PERSONAL VALUES	1	2	3	4	5

Accomplishment _____
Acknowledgement _____
Challenge _____
Cooperation _____
Creativity _____
Expertise _____
Friendship _____
Honesty _____
Independence _____
Instruction _____
Intimacy _____
Responsibility _____
Organization _____
Pleasure _____
Quality _____
Recognition _____
Security _____
Tranquility _____
Empathy _____
Variety _____
Wealth _____

Values Interpretation Chart

VALUE	PRIMARY NEED	RELATED FEAR
Accomplishment	Achievement	Failure
Acknowedgement	Appreciation	Being Unappreciated
Challenge	Stimulation	Stagnation
Cooperation	Unity	Dissension
Creativity	To Express Self	Repression
Expertise	To Feel Competent	Incompetent, Ordinary
Friendship	To Influence Others	Being Separated
Honesty	Trust	Deception

Value	Primary Need	Related Fear
Independence	Be In Self Control	Being Controlled
Instruction	Understanding	Confusion
Intimacy	Close To Another	Emotionally Alone
Organization	Order	Chaos
Pleasure	Play, Entertainment	Boredom
Quality	High Standards	Low Standards
Recognition	Attention	Being Ignored
Responsibility	In Control	Not In Control
Security	Peace Of Mind	Being In Debt
Tranquility	Harmony	Conflict
Empathy	Feelings Understood	Feelings Ignored
Variety	Experience	Routine
Wealth	Rewards	Poverty

Developed by C.R.G ltd.

Above and beyond the already mentioned motivational ideas are four easy-to-implement special motivational strategies discussed below.

Redesigning the Job

Jobs need to be designed so that the worker (a) is given the responsibility and challenge that matches his/her skills, abilities, aptitudes, and expectations; (b) can experience a wholeness to his/her work; (c) can more easily identify his/her contributions to the organization's objectives; (d) can participate in decisions that affect his/her job, and (e) control larger proportions of his/her own work.

Job redesign involves redefining the job. Employees are given greater responsibility, allowed more control, and provided frequent feedback. There are two broad aspects in job redesign; job enlargement and job restructuring.

Job enlargement increases the number of tasks assigned to the employee. The employee's decision-making authority or skill level is not increased. So the quality of the work is not necessarily changing, rather the quantity.

Job restructuring involves changing the quality of the work that is required of the individual. It's an attempt to increase the depth of the job by requiring higher areas of knowledge and skill. In some cases it can give the employees added opportunity for planning and controlling their work. The idea is simple: employees can manage themselves quite well if they're allowed to. Jobs are expanded to allow workers to participate in managerial functions in which traditionally they had no input, functions like planning and controlling. Employees use their own judgement and discretion to make decisions about their work. They participate with their supervisors in problem-solving and goal-setting. They offer an array of ideas, suggestions, and personal opinions. The employee is given greater autonomy and increased responsibility for planning, directing, and controlling the work done.

To facilitate employees' suggestions, you can establish an employee suggestion box. Taking the time to ask employees what they think, soliciting their recommendations and acting upon them, (or giving them a solid reason why we cannot act upon their suggestions at this particular time), in itself, can be a very motivating activity.

Job Rotation

Job rotation is similar to cross-training: employees switch from one job to another. It provides employees with experience in different jobs on a regular basis. The jobs can be rotated within or between departments. Job rotation provides variety and helps prevent boredom. It also helps the organization reduce the risk of down time if you have staff that are trained on several different positions. If someone is ill and has to be away from his/her position for a while, you have two or three other people that are trained to do it.

Job Sharing

Job sharing is having two or three people sharing one full-time position. My sister-in-law, a public health nurse, job-shares her position with another nurse. They split the week, one working two days, the other working three days, then they switch the following week. They each work about 20 hours a week, providing them a part-time permanent position. This works well for them as they both have young children and don't want to be away from them on a full-time basis. They are able to maintain an active involvement in their careers and keep their skills fresh. The additional income is also beneficial. Likewise, this arrangement helped their employer by providing a workable solution to government cutbacks that would have eliminated a couple of full-time positions. By creating one full-time position shared by two part-time staff, both nurses were able to keep their jobs. In the end, everyone wins.

Flex-Time

Flex-time allows employees to work schedules that consist of two time parts. The first time part is a base period often called the core time. That's when everyone must be at work The second time is the flexible component, usually at the beginning or the ending period of each work shift. Employees can choose their arrival and departure time. Flex-time allows the night owls as well as the early birds to work the hours during which they're most sharp. It also accommodates additional obligations such as family schedules and other job commitments.

The use of flex-time programs is definitely growing throughout North America. In 1977, only 15 percent of companies surveyed had flex-time programs. By1985, an AMS survey of 280 U.S. companies showed that 28 percent were using flex-time and another five percent were considering a flex-time program. Some of the most prestigious corporations in Corporate America have successful flex-time programs. At Hewlett-Packard, employees can start to work at 6 AM, 7 AM, or 8 AM. Control Data notes that tardiness and absenteeism decreased since the introduction of flex-time. Fox, Jones, and Associates, a company of consultants in Toronto, Ontario, Canada, has a unique plan. Employee benefits include as much vacation as the employee wants. The founder, Jeremy Fox, feels the policy actually increases productivity, encouraging employees to organize their time more efficiently, project by project, rather than day by day.

The Metropolitan Life Insurance Company of New York, a flex-time employer since 1974, reports increased productivity when workers schedule their own hours. Conneco, in Houston, Texas, switched to flex-time in 1976. People arrive as early as 6:45 AM so they can get a lot done prior to the telephone starting to ring. Meredith, the Des Moines-based publisher of magazines such as *Better Homes and Gardens* and *Metropolitan Home*, uses flex-time in the office and compresses the work week in the press rooms.

Another trend that we started to see in the early 1990's is people being allowed to work out of their home. Through the use of the fax machines, E-Mail, and periodic meetings, many people are simply turning the spare bedroom in their house into an office. They work out of the home even though they are fully employed by a corporation.

Some of the specific benefits to flex-time-type strategies are: improved employee attitude and morale; accommodation of the working parent and child care arrangements; increases in productivity; decreases in absenteeism and tardiness; accommodation of those who wish to arrive at work before interruptions such as the phone begin; facilitation of scheduling employees' medical, dental, and other appointments; accommodation of employees' leisure-time activities; and decreases in turnover.

In short, I am saying that when it comes to staff motivation, cash is definitely not king. Money is not the answer to dealing with problems of poor morale, low productivity, or high absenteeism. Today's employees require more: a real commitment and a sense of loyalty from the organization. They want and need to be involved in the decision-making process. They need an opportunity for advancement, personal growth, and challenge. They require all the things just covered in this chapter, and they need them on a consistent basis. If you're not prepared to fulfill these requirements regularly, after a while what you're going to have is "sick" employees. And a sick employee can easily be seen. It's one who is demotivated, dissatisfied with the position and disenchanted. The net result is low productivity and high turnover. We know the phenomenal cost of hiring and training great staff. So the key is to pay a little bit now. If you're not prepared to pay a little now to keep your great people, then it's going to cost you a whole lot more in the end.

Chapter Four

BECOMING AN EXCEPTIONAL LEADER

Let's get rid of management. I think one of the most significant things that corporate America can do during the turbulent and highly competitive 1990's is to get rid of management. What do I mean by this?

I really believe that staff in the 1990's don't want to be managed. They want to be led. Whoever heard of a "world manager?" A "world leader," sure. An education leader? Yes. A political leader, a religious leader, a sports leader, a community leader, a labour leader, a business leader, a retail leader . . . the point is these people lead, they don't manage.

The carrot always wins over the stick. Ask your horse. As the clichés say, "You can **lead** your horse to water, but you cannot **manage** him to drink." "If you want to manage somebody, manage yourself." If you do that well, you'll be ready to stop managing and start leading.

One of the problems of putting all the focus into **managing** people, as opposed to **leading** people is that it relies too much on the manager's ability to supervise over staff and not allow the staff to be accountable for their own actions. I think, rather, it makes a lot more sense if you hire good people, orient and train them and create a motivational climate from which they can grow and learn. Then the people can manage themselves. I think the key to effective leadership in the '90's is to lead the organization in a manner that allows everyone to manage themselves.

My definition of leadership is, *"the ability to turn a dream or a vision of a desired future state into a reality with the support and assistance of other people."*

Another way to look at leadership is to compare it to gardening. Gardeners use sunlight, water, and fertilizer to turn seeds into wonderful plants. Leaders use communication, self-esteem, vision and their own personal level of enthusiasm to grow wonderful people who achieve personal and organizational goals. Leaders, then, can be seen as the gardeners of corporate America. As Bernard Montgomery once said, *"The true test of leadership is the feeling that people have after a chat with you."* By this he means that if after speaking to you (the leader) they have a feeling of uplift and confidence, you have succeeded as a leader. A little later in this chapter I'll talk more about how a leader can be like a gardener and I will provide the specific strategies on how to emulate both leader and gardner.

Before I go further, there are six myths of leadership that I want to dispell:

Leadership Myth Number 1

The first myth is that leadership in itself is a rare skill. I don't think this is true at all. In fact, as I look around, I see all sorts of day-to-day examples of leadership in practice. For example, you can go to your average ice hockey rink and see all sorts of parents volunteering their time after hours, on the weekends, and at the wee hours of the morning, leading youngsters in games of hockey. You see it on the baseball field, in swimming pools, gymnasiums, dance halls, everywhere. That's only one example. There are also examples of people getting involved in a number of leadership roles within a volunteer organization, like the president of the local Toastmaster's Chapter. They could also be leading a fund-raising drive for the Heart and Stroke Foundation or some other charitable organization. I think you need to take the time to look around at pure leadership roles. You'll find that indeed there is an abundance of these skills. The challenge is to learn how to transfer these leadership abilities we use in other facets of our lives, and apply them to our business lives.

Leadership Myth Number 2

Another common leadership myth is that leaders are born, and not made. I believe that it's a combination of our life experiences—our environment—as well as our reference groups—people like our parents, our siblings, our friends, the whole education system, religious organizations and the media. All of these combine and create what I call the Reference Groups. Now our Reference Groups become a critical part of our environment. The things that we're exposed to at a young age have a tremendous impact on how we perceive the world. I really believe that leaders are not born; rather, they are created as a result of their experiences and their expectations of life, as well as what they've learned from their Reference Groups.

Leadership Myth Number 3

That leadership is the same as management is another myth. In short, I think managers attempt to do things right—according to rules, policies, regulations, and systems—and leaders simply try to do the right thing. I see management as the day-to-day supervision of the systems and the people of an organization, while I see leadership as the deliberate energy that is put into an organization to get all the players to jump together as a cohesive team and propel them forward towards the stated short and long-term goals of the organization.

Leadership Myth Number 4

The fourth myth, that leadership only exists at the top of an organization, I don't think is accurate at all. In some cases, there isn't a lot of leadership at the top of an organization, but leadership is pervasive throughout the organization. For example, you can be looking at a shop steward who represents the union. This person might be sitting at the bottom of the actual hierarchy chart of the organization, but has real and legitimate power and a *bona fide* leadership role as a shop steward.

There are leaders within the department, leaders within divisions, leaders within workgroups, and leaders in various projects that are taken on within an organization. So, I believe that leadership is not a function of someone sitting on the corporate totem pole; rather, leadership is the person making a conscious decision to take an active role within the organization.

Leadership Myth Number 5

Myth number five—leadership power is a bad or dangerous thing. I don't think power is either a good thing or a bad thing, but what you do with power is what puts a slant on it. If you have honorable intentions to do positive things within the organization and with a few individuals that you're trying to propel through it, then I say that power base is actually a positive thing. Now if you're going to use your power for personal greed or to do a hostile takeover of the corporation, then I see your use of power as negative.

But as I said, leadership power is definitely not a bad thing in my estimation. In fact, quite the contrary. As leaders, you need to deliberately attempt to expand your personal power base. Because what is power? Power is really the ability to influence others. And one of the things that you're trying to do is influence the majority of individuals within the organization to come on board and share your common vision and with you lead the company in the direction that you feel the company needs to go.

Leadership Myth Number 6

The sixth leadership myth is that leaders are created by extraordinary or great events, and that there must be a shocking or traumatic occurrence to propel them into the position of leadership. Well, you've certainly read about those cases. But there are many unsung heroes, day-to-day leaders that weren't catapulted into this position. There wasn't any traumatic event that led them to become leaders; rather, it was their own daily dissatisfaction with the events within a current industry or organization that prompted them to take certain actions. As a result, the road they chose led them to the top and they assumed the leadership position.

To be an effective leader in today's business world, you need to possess most, if not all, of the following 10 Dominant Characteristics:

1. Dominant Characteristics: Sense of Purpose

The first dominant characteristic is what I call a strong sense of **purpose**. By this I mean that you have a burning desire from within. I'll give you a couple of examples. Thomas Edison is known as one of the most prolific inventors of all time. Apparently, he had a hard time with his invention of the light bulb. The trouble was with the development of the filament, the little part inside the bulb that would heat up and glow, creating light. He tried thousands of different combinations of materials to get the filament right, and the thing would either not light up at all or would light up too quickly and explode.

Well, one night, as the story goes, he was expressing some of his frustration with his experiments to a colleague, when a young man who had been listening to the conversation interjected: "Pardon me, Mr. Edison, sorry for interrupting, but as I listen to you recount your trials and tribulations with this experiment, it strikes me that you failed about 2,000 times to figure out how this thing's going to work, so why don't you just give up? Your valuable time is better used doing something else."

Well, Edison thought about this for a moment, looked at the young man, and replied: "Young man, you don't understand much about the ways of the world. You see, I did not fail 2,000 times. Rather, I was successful in learning 2,000 ways that this will not work. Which means I am that much closer to finding out the way that it will work."

This illustrates a very important point—that one of the true characteristics of the effective leader is a very strong sense of purpose. It's what I call the burning desire in the pit of the stomach.

Another example is Henry Ford. Back in the 1920's, when everyone else was making a few cars, he said, "Well, what if I could produce a car and make it dependable and everything else that the consumer wanted. If I could produce enough of those, I could make a lot of money as well as take care of the transportation requirements for the vast majority of Americans."

So, he went out and talked to a number of Americans, American consumers, and said, "Listen, would you be looking for an automobile?" And then he told them a number of different physical characteristics on safety, and how fast it should go, and the liability, and so on and so forth. He brought all the findings back to his team of engineers, mechanics and designers and said, "Okay, I need you to build this car." And they said, "No problem at all. We can build that." But Mr. Ford added, "We have to be able to build it for this amount of money." They looked at him and said, "You're nuts! It can't be done." They were not used to building several cars at a time. So Mr. Ford fired them all, and hired a whole new set of engineers, designers, and mechanics, and he said to them, "We need to build a car that's going to meet these requirements, these specifications. We have to produce it for this amount of money so that we can turn it around, raise the price a little bit, and sell it for this amount of money to the general public. The general public will be prepared to pay this amount of money, but not anything more."

Because of this burning desire, this personal belief that the Ford Company could do it, Henry Ford surrounded himself with similar people who accepted his vision. In turn, they changed the rules. They created a whole new methodology for building cars— the assembly line: mass production.

I think the major point of difference between the average person and the leader is that the average person cannot believe it until he/she sees it. Whereby the leader says, "If I believe it, then I'll see it." It's having that passion, that sense of purpose, that makes a leader of an ordinary person.

With more than eight years of experience training people in leadership principles, I've studied thousands of men and women from all walks of life. My research has brought about many interesting facts about purpose that I would like to share with you.

One of the most striking facts is that those who have succeeded in their endeavors applied common principles very effectively. In turn, these people became uncommon leaders in their various fields. One funny thing about common sense though, is that it's not that common anymore.

You know, it's not enough for people to have education, intelligence, or the ability to succeed. Thousands of leaders throughout the world have all these traits but still fail, or produce at performance levels far lower than their potential. Why? Because they lack worthy ambition. People without a purpose never leave a mark on the land. They're lost in the mass of people, and they do not bring out their true talents and potential. Whatever initial advantages these people may have, without the primary principal purpose, they become poor—or at best average—at the performance. Life is too short for any one of us to accomplish everything. However, some of us, if we apply our potential, can accomplish more than one thing well in our lives. Many, in fact, can accomplish at least one important worthy purpose in life if we set our minds to do so.

Success comes to those leaders who have a definite purpose in their lives and are supported by practical written plans of action and strategies of how they're going to accomplish this. I think we all must have a specific mission which can contribute positively to other people. And I believe that this primary mission needs to be bigger and broader than our own self. The following questions can get us thinking about our life mission:

What do you want out of life?

What is your life mission?

What becomes of you when you have achieved your life's mission?

Which category out of the following six categories are you striving to accomplish?

> The challenge of life.
>
> The love for people.
>
> The well-being of others.
>
> Their personal wealth.
>
> The power over other people.
>
> The status of personal health and well-being.

Can your present job help you achieve this major goal?

Do you have a well-written plan to work towards this major goal?

It is only when you can answer the above questions truthfully that you will be able to aim for something meaningful in life. Don't settle for a mere mediocre sort of existence. Don't measure yourself by your past failures or achievements, nor by your present abilities.

Make as your purpose in life a cause more important than yourself. For example, take Japanese Doctor Yushero Nagamatz—a very famous inventor. To date he's registered more than 2,360 patents to his name. He does this by working 9 AM to midnight each day in his life. Dr. Nagamatz says, "I have a mission to accomplish in life. Japan is very short of any resources, beyond people, water and fish, and must import all goods critical to industry. Therefore, if we don't create, we shall die."

With such a purpose in his life, it is little wonder that he has been inducted into the International Inventors' Hall of Fame by the Inventors' Club of America, and he has won the Blue Ribbon Award for inventors.

Another example, Mother Teresa, has a life mission—to help poor people in India who are sick and dying by the thousands. When she first started her personal crusade, she faced many problems and obstacles. But today, she has initiated many hospitals, schools, and places of dwelling for the poor of India. A Nobel Peace Prize winner, she has said, "Each one of us has a mission to fulfill, our mission of love. At the hour of death, when we come face to face with God, we are measured by love. Not how much we have done, but how much we have loved, and how much love we have put into our actions."

The burning desire to achieve your ambitions is such a strong, deep, emotional urge of wanting to achieve a worthy goal that you are prepared to pay any price to achieve it. Exceptional leaders possess strong willpower to get what they want, and they're willing to pay the price in advance to get it. Therefore, they succeed in achieving their goals. Most people wish for many things, but they're not willing to pay the price for what they want. Hence, they give up when faced with problems and obstacles and invariably sabotage their success.

Achievement leaders possess backbones, whereas failure is spineless. A strong willpower to win is reflected by one of my colleagues, W. Mitchell. He is a professional speaker who tours around the country with a very simple message, simple, yet very powerful. "It's not what happens to you, it's what you do about it."

Some 20 years ago, young Mitchell was working in San Francisco on the trolley cars. After a while, he came up with some money and bought himself a new motorbike. As he was travelling through San Francisco on his motorbike, a delivery truck cut him off causing a horrible accident. At the point when he was skidding along the ground and the sparks were flying from metal hitting the pavement, something happened. The cap from the gas tank popped off the motorcycle, the sparks ignited the gas and poor

Mitchell's body was burnt instantaneously. Several days later, when he awoke at the hospital, he was in unbelievable pain and agony from the burns to 90 percent of his body, he was all bandaged up, and he had broken a number of bones.

After several weeks of soul-searching and going through the "Why me, Lord?" syndrome, he decided that he wasn't going to dwell on the negative, but rather say to himself, "Well, what do I do now? What do I wait for?"

Several years later, he decided to open up a business called Vermont Castings. Now Vermont Castings had quickly grown to be one of the world's leading producers and exporters of wood-burning stoves. Mitchell was a major shareholder and a founder of this company. He's done very well. Then, a couple of years ago, he was flying his small aircraft with two friends around Colorado where they had a freakish accident. His small propellor plane crashed into a mountainside. While his two friends were able to walk away from the wreck, he was an instant paraplegic. Upon this, his wife, unable to deal with this tragedy, left him. Again, he went through all the agony of what I call, "The Victim Mentality" saying, "Why, Lord? Why has this happened to me? This is such a terrible thing. I feel terrible." However after a while, he decided to focus on what he did have versus what he didn't have.

With that in mind, he later became the Mayor of a small community in Colorado. He took on a major mining exploration company that wanted to exploit the natural resources of a nearby mountain, and became known as the man who saved the mountain. He also ran for State Governor and, although he didn't win, he came in a close second. He now tours all over the world with his very motivational subject, entitled *"It's not what happens to you, it's what you do about it."* I think his message is very powerful; it needs to be heard by many, many people.

W. Mitchell's strong willpower to win is a definite indicator of someone who's a true inspiration to us all; he is definitely a contemporary leader of the '90's.

How can we take the burning desire that we all have within us and multiply it? Well, there are two proven techniques. One is called *Creative Visualization*, and another method is called *Positive Affirmation Statements*.

With *Creative Visualization*, what you're doing is creating a mental picture of yourself achieving your goal to become the kind of person and leader that you want. If you perform this mental exercise, this visualization in your mind, for two or three minutes every night before going to sleep and every morning before you get up, you will see yourself actually being more successful in becoming the leader that you want to become, and having the impact on your followers that you want to have. You will also create an emotional link with this success.

Another tool is *Positive Affirmation Statements*. This is talking about your own level of selftalk, to program yourself with more confidence in your own abilities. You can do this to remind yourself when you say, "I am a great leader. I am a visionary." See it in your mind and repeat it over and over again. What you end up doing is creating and planting a number of positive thoughts in the subconscious mind so that you actually move towards success more rapidly.

2. Dominant Characteristic: Persistence

The second dominant characteristic of an effective leader is persistence. There's a great example of this. Towards the latter part of World War II, in the United Kingdom, Sir Winston Churchill gathered a number of people. He was going to make a speech. The German Air Force was bombing London and the surrounding area, almost winning the air battle.

At this point Churchill decided that he needed to inspire his people to get them excited and working towards one goal. He told them the key to succeeding was persistence. He summed up one of his most famous speeches with a very short but powerful conclusion: "Never give up. Never, never give up." In those seven words Sir Winston Churchill epitomized the power of persistence; to create a sense of the unstoppable.

Brian Tracy, professional speaker and author of the best-selling Nightingale-Conant audio cassette, says, "To create an *unstoppable mindset*, leaders must be persistent." Former president Hubert Hoover said, "Nothing in the world can take the place of persistence. Talent will not: nothing is more common than unsuccessful people with talent. Genius will not: unrewarded genius is almost a proverb. Education will not: the world is full of educated derelicts. The slogan 'Press on' has solved—and always will solve—the problems of the human race."

3. Dominant Characteristic: Self-knowledge

The third dominant characteristic of an effective leader is being self-knowledgeable. You know what your strengths are, you know what your weaknesses are. It's like the following assessment form called "Leadership Characteristic Personal Assessment Form." It's a quick instrument to find out where your strengths and weaknesses lie within leadership. Once in a while you have to take an accurate and honest account of what you're good at and the areas in your life that are weak, and identify the weak areas that need to be worked on.

Leadership Characteristic Personal Assessment Form

(-)		(+)	Score
1. Weak sense of purpose	1 2 3 4 5 6 7	Strong sense of purpose	___
2. Gives up easily	1 2 3 4 5 6 7	Very persistent	___
3. No self-awareness	1 2 3 4 5 6 7	Self-knowledgeable	___
4. Doesn't acquire new skills, information	1 2 3 4 5 6 7	Always seeking new learning	___
5. Bored, apathetic in relation to work	1 2 3 4 5 6 7	Sense of pleasure, joy in relation to work	___
6. Unable to attract others	1 2 3 4 5 6 7	Magnetic, draws others	___
7. Treats others with minimal respect, caring	1 2 3 4 5 6 7	Mature in human relationships	___
8. Fearful of the new, the unproven	1 2 3 4 5 6 7	Takes risk, likes to experiment	___
9. Depressed, discouraged by mistakes	1 2 3 4 5 6 7	Sees mistakes as opportunities	___
10. Self-ambitious; focused on own wants	1 2 3 4 5 6 7	Seeks to serve needs of others	___

TOTAL SCORE _____

BECOMING AN EXCEPTIONAL LEADER 117

Once you have completed the Leadership Characteristic Personal Assessment Form, total up your points. If you scored between 10 and 45, you will benefit greatly from this program and the attitudes it will help you develop. If you scored between 50 and 60, this program will help you sharpen your already strong leadership abilities. If you score above 60 you're in great shape, but will nonetheless benefit from the scientific presentation of the techniques we offer in this SyberVision program.

4. Dominant Characteristic: The Learning Mindset

The fourth dominant characteristic of an effective leader is to have what I call "The Learning Mindset." You have to have a student mentality. The following diagram shows the four levels of learning.

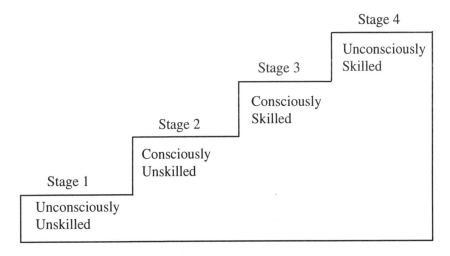

4 Levels of Learning

The bottom level of learning is called "Unconsciously Unskilled." In the Unconscious/Unskilled stage of learning, you are not aware that you do not know. Then at some point, someone brings it to your attention that you do not know. So then you now become conscious of the fact that you are unskilled, and then you move into Stage 2, where you become "Consciously Unskilled."

At this point, you are bothered by the fact that you do not know, so you start to do something about it. You take courses, you read books, you learn. And then you move into Stage 3, where you now become "Consciously Skilled." This can be a very dangerous stage. This is what I often call "The Brightest Stage." At this stage, you believe that you know everything that there is to know about the subject of which you're talking. Obviously, if you start to believe that you know everything about the subject matter, you're going to stop investing yourself, and you're going to stop learning. I think one of the key things here is to get out of this state. It's enough to remember that the good Lord provided you with two ears and only one mouth, so that you may listen twice as much as you speak.

What do I mean by this? I really believe that when I'm speaking, I'm not learning. As soon as I take the time to close my mouth and listen, then I can learn. What you need to do is to have the "Student Mentality" as I mentioned before. The "Student Mentality" says, "Hey, sure I know a little bit about the subject matter, but I'm always seeking more information, I'm always trying to learn more about the subject."

And that leads into Stage 4. If you are the true master, you're constantly seeking to learn more, constantly immersing yourself in additional knowledge, eventually you will become unconsciously skilled. You know your unconscious skills when, for example, you're playing goalie in an ice hockey game, and all of a sudden there's a flurry of action, and you've lost sight of who has the puck. Then out of your peripheral vision you see the puck racing toward you. Purely out of instinct you shoot up your glove to deflect the puck. That's an example of someone who has become a master. The person has trained so much, learned so much about the technique, and has created an unconscious reflex that, in this case, will prevent a goal from being scored.

5. Dominant Characteristic: Joy in Work

The fifth dominant characteristic of an effective leader is that effective leaders don't see themselves as going to work. Rather, they have a total sense of pleasure and joy in relation to their work. That's why they're able to expend such a phenomenal amount of time and energy into their careers. They don't see it as going to work. In many cases, they see it as going to play, and they just happen to get paid for playing. You have to have an absolute passion for what you do in order to be the very best at it. In my estimation if you are used to staring at the clock, punching out at 5:00 PM sharp, and all that nine-to-five mentality, then you can never truly become an effective leader. To rise above the mediocrity of life and be a successful leader, you must be a person of action; you must be willing to work with consistent and continuous effort.

Chief Justice Harold E. Hughes put it very clearly by saying, "I believe in work. Hard work and long hours of work. No one has a break down from overwork, but from worry and inactivity."

Extraordinary leaders are actually ordinary people who put in extraordinary effort in their pursuit of excellence. Many people do not like their work, and only some people like their work moderately. There are very few who actually love their work. For example, labourers usually toil with an indifferent attitude, while great artists create their work with unquenchable passion and care. When you're engaged in work you love, you can invest long hours without feeling tired or fatigued. You become most efficient and you succeed better when you love your work and are committed and dedicated to your loved ones, organization, and country.

6. Dominant Characteristic: Golden Rule

The sixth dominant characteristic of an effective leader is the application of the Golden Rule in human relationships. In short, what I'm saying here is that the effective leader seeks to develop loving, nurturing, supportive relationships with other humans. The Golden Rule in human relationships states, "Do unto others as you want others to do unto you." In Christianity, Jesus said, "All things whatsoever that men should do to you, do so to them." In Islam, "No one of you is a believer until you desire for his brother that which he has desired for himself." In Buddhism, "Hurt not others in ways that you yourself would find hurtful." In Hinduism, "Do not unto others that which would cause you pain if done unto you."

There are always references to the "self-made leader." In fact, there's no such thing as the self-made leader, because no leader has ever made it to the top without the help of other people. It has been said, "He rises highest who helps others to rise." Just like milk, you can never stop the cream from rising to the top. You can never rise above mediocrity until you possess distinguished hallmarks of effective leadership. In business, sports, or in personal life, there's going to be ups and there's going to be downs. It's when you're down and sometimes out that you need your friends.

All these metaphors may sound cliché but the truth is you need friends to encourage you and help you come up again. Even if you're a leader of a group of people, you need a collective and united effort to achieve your goal as well as the group members' own personal goals. This is only possible when you're able to assert a friendly and effective relationship with each and every one of them in order to build a unified team. You can be rich only when you enrich the lives of other people. You only learn the meaning of living when you can surrender your ego to the service of your fellow person. In order to be of sincere interest to others, you must first be a sincere friend. As a colleague of mine, founder of the National Speakers' Association, Cavett Robert has often said, "No one cares how much you know until you know how much you care." You can live in history when you think more of your friends than of yourself, your country rather than your bank book. Real and true friends will follow you anywhere; through the brightness and the darkness, through the shadows and the sunlight. Ask yourself these thought-provoking questions: How many true friends, and not just social friends, do I really have? Who are they? Do they believe in me? Do they encourage me to become an outstanding leader in my specialized field? Will they lend me a helping hand, or even two hands, if I need it? Do they encourage me and motivate me to achieve my goals in life?

Here are some useful tips that can help you apply the Golden Rule principle and develop true friendship, co-operation, and support other people as you become an even more effective leader.

a. Be more lovable to your loved ones. Spend quality time in meaningful activities with them.

b. Be more concerned about your fellow workers and help them achieve their personal goals. Introduce a more caring attitude for them by letting them participate in the decision-making process, by making them feel a part of the organization.

c. Associate with successful people, particularly those that are the leaders in your profession and industry. In my case, if I want to become even more successful as a professional speaker, I need close personal friends who are well-known professional speakers. I have asked people like Bill Gibson, Brian Tracy, and Og Mandino to personally be my *mentor*. And then you learn from their experiences.

d. Apply "The customer comes first" and "The customer is always right" principles to your clientele. Always be prepared to serve them sincerely and efficiently.

The Servant

"Humility recognizes that the only master there is on earth is a servant. All those who seek to become masters fail. So few are seeking to become servants, and it is the servant whom others eventually call **master**. This is true of everyone who at sometime or another has been named master. The master is always working twenty hours a day while the disciple is sleeping his eight hours and enjoying holidays."

—Bill Gibson

e. Form a team of professionals in various specialized skills to advise and support you to achieve your mission. These experts may include: a doctor, a dentist, a lawyer, a banker, a tax accountant, a business investment consultant, a spiritual adviser, a personal confidante, your own success coach/mentor, or an insurance agent.

7. Dominant Characteristic: Calculated Risks

The seventh dominant characteristic of an effective leader is that the leader takes calculated risks and is prepared to experiment. The leader is prepared —as they say in *Star Trek*— "To boldly go where no one has gone before." This is not to say, take unnecessary, dangerous tangents; rather look at the whole opportunity, size up the situation, and say "Okay, can I take a calculated risk here?"

8. Dominant Characteristic: Opportunities

The eighth dominant characteristic of an effective leader is someone who sees mistakes as opportunities. Basically, it's how you choose to see the world. Are you going to look at every little setback or every little obstacle as a failure, and then remind yourself that you failed in that area? Or are you going to look at all these times that maybe you weren't as successful as you would have liked to have been, as learning opportunities, and an opportunity for you to go forward?

9. Dominant Characteristic: Living Magnet

The ninth dominant characteristic is what I call "becoming the living magnet." I sincerely believe that you draw people, places, and circumstances into your life that are consistent with your dominant thoughts. So if you are a very positive, upbeat, pro-active, successful person, you will draw those types of people into your life, and into your organization. I think there's a real magnetism or charisma that is exuded by the effective leader. And this doesn't necessarily have to be done in a very loud or forceful manner. You can take a very quiet, self-assured priest, or an individual like Mahatma Ghandi, now there's someone who exuded all sorts of personal power and charisma without having to raise his voice or lift a loaded weapon. It's like a magnet that draws people in towards you. And one of the things of course, for the leader, is he/she has to have a sufficient number of followers to help move the leaders towards his/her stated goals.

10. Dominant Characteristic: Serve Others

The last dominant characteristic of the effective leader is that he/she seeks constantly to serve the needs of other people. What you want to accomplish in the long run is the empowerment of every individual within the organization to the degree that everyone is actually managing his/her day-to-day action as each individual moves towards the long-term objectives of the organization. But how do we get to this stage? The Leadership Success Chart following the survey specifically explains how leaders can empower individuals within their organization.

A Survey

A survey conducted by the firm that produced *Lead, Follow, or Get Out of the Way* asked over two thousand managers to list the characteristics that contributed to their respect for leaders.

Characteristics of Leaders (in order of frequency listed)	% of Responses
1. Communicates, allows input, is willing to listen.	11
2. Is interested, appreciative, complimentary, supportive, humanistic, considerate.	10
3. Displays honesty, integrity, trustworthiness.	10
4. Is objective, open-minded, tolerant, rational, reasonable, and fair.	9
5. Delegates, trusts subordinates, allows room to achieve.	8
6. Motivates, challenges, inspires, is team-oriented.	7
7. Is knowledgeable, experienced, competent, intelligent, has good judgment.	6
8. Is available, approachable; provides feedback; trains, coaches.	5
9. Is constructive, enthusiastic, positive, friendly, humorous.	5
10. Is decisive, courageous; takes risks; is willing to commit.	5
11. Is goal-oriented, makes plans, clarifies expectations, follows through.	4

12.	Accepts responsibility, blame; admits errors; is respected, respectful.	3
13.	Is a doer, participates, sets example.	3
14.	Is open, candid, sincere, credible.	3
15.	Is tactful, humble, sensitive, understanding.	3
16.	Sets high standards; is dedicated, hard-working, reliable.	3
17.	Is consistent, even-tempered.	3
18.	Is organized, structured.	2
19.	Is creative, resourceful; has vision.	1
20.	Other.	1

Leadership Success Chart

Starting on the far left-hand side of the diagram, with "Vision." Vision + Communications + Positioning + Self-Management = Empowerment of the individual in the organization. Well, what does this mean? This can be seen as taking the time to paint a mental picture of a desired state into your minds. Now your vision can come from the mission statement of the organization. John F. Kennedy had a vision in the early 60's to have an American on the moon by the end of the decade. Martin Luther King had a vision as well, that was expressed in his slogan, "I have a dream."

By taking the time to help your followers paint a mental picture of the desired statement in their minds, you're going to add an awful lot more power and conviction behind the mission, behind the objective. When JFK created the vision of an American on the moon, he used all sorts of visual aids to help people buy into this vision. Throughout NASA, there were pictures and symbols of the moon and of lunar exploration, and various pieces of apparatus were left around so people could look at them and visually connect in their minds with the purpose and the dominant theme that was bringing them together in the organization and propelling them forward.

There are seven key points that leaders strive to communicate to their followers. The first is their absolute **passion** for their vision. This is expressed by the leader's energy, by his/her commitment, and by his/her own modelling of the desired state. They are living the model, as it were.

The second point is leaders want their vision to be **understood** by all people, by all of their followers. Thirdly, the leader wants everyone within the organization to understand what's in it for each one of them. In other words, what the **benefits** are to each person in being successful in achieving his/her vision. The fourth point is that leaders seek to communicate **solidarity** and clarity and unison from top management down. The fifth point is that leaders strive to draw in all their staff to the vision so that they are **committed** in striving towards the achievement of the long-term goal. The sixth point, leaders also seek to communicate **action** so that the team will be propelled into action. And lastly, the one I think is the real test here, is that **interpersonal communications**, the relationship between the leader and the followers, will be strengthened.

Sometimes there are barriers that, unless you deal with them, will prevent you from being 100 percent successful in achieving your stated vision. They could be internal barriers, external barriers, or relationship barriers.

Internal barriers can be the actual structural recording systems that are used within the organization. External barriers can be legislation, problems with suppliers, or any other difficulties with clients that could prevent us from achieving our vision. And lastly, probably the most complex barrier is the relationship between the various team players within the organization. What you need to do is find out what obstacles lie within your path and resolve to overcome them and work directly towards success.

A key component in leadership success is self-management. If every individual within the organization is held personally accountable for managing him/herself and is given the tools and the latitude to manage him/herself effectively, then no one needs to worry about managing another individual. That would free up the leader's time to do more effective things such as acting as a coach and mentor and leader, rather than playing the role of supervisor and manager.

Five Basic Styles Of Leadership

There are **five basic styles of leadership** which most leaders use or have available for use. They are:

1. *Directive*—This is a fairly **autocratic style of leadership**. When using this style, the leader relies heavily on one-way, downward communication with followers. He or she "tells" the employee

precisely what to do, when and how to do it, where it should be done and all other details of the task.

Advantages—It is quick, easy to use and sometimes efficient.

Disadvantages—People generally do not like being "told" what to do without explanation. There is little room for questioning to avoid misunderstanding. The better way might be overlooked. It detracts from positive human relations practice. Can tie up a lot of leader's time in follow-up.

2. *Persuasive*—this is **a "selling" style.** Here, the leader still is quite directive, as above. Now, though, he or she takes the time to explain why the instruction is "best" and to answer questions.

   Advantages—Still quick and easy. Slightly better human relations impact. Can be efficient.

   Disadvantages—Still does not obtain real commitment. Better way can still be overlooked. Can be seen as manipulation. Still ties up leader's time in follow-up.

3. *Consultative*—At this point, **the leader is willing to sincerely obtain input from followers before making a final decision.** The leader usually will state the issue or problem and ask followers for their opinions or suggestions. After listening to the inputs, the leader then decides and acts.

   Advantages—Better follower involvement. Greater acceptance of decision. Improves decision accuracy. Reasonably easy and efficient. Communication is two-way.

   Disadvantages—Can be a more time consuming process. Requires greater skill on leader's part than earlier styles. Can give rise to impatience on follower's part and even to feelings that leader is weak; e.g., relies too heavily on others for decisions.

4. *Participative*—Now **the leader actually gives up part of his or her decision making power.** The leader invites employees to fully participate and together with the leader jointly reach a decision. The final outcome is a true consensus decision.

   Advantages—Enhances acceptance and commitment to the decision by followers. Decisions tend to be more accurate and of better all-around quality. Improves flow of two-way communication.

Builds trust. Develops followers' skills.

Disadvantages—Can be very slow and time consuming. Requires considerable leader skill. Can have limited application. Sometimes leads to work group frustration—especially if consensus is not achieved.

5. *Delegative*—In this style, **the leader turns over (delegates) the entire matter to the followers for their decision.** He or she is mainly interested in results—less so about how the results are attained.

Advantages—Also quick, easy to use and relatively efficient since leader's time is kept free. Fosters follower growth and development. Strong follower acceptance and commitment.

Disadvantages—Risky. Dangerous if followers are not sufficiently trained or skilled. Does not foster improved human relations or communications since contact between leader and followers is at "arm's length."

Five Keys to Self-Management

There are five keys to self-management—and this applies to any level of the organization, to any position within the organization.

1. Key to Self-Management: Positivement Mental Attitude

You need to develop a **positive mental attitude**. In other words, it's how you choose to see the world. Do you see the world as being a relatively negative place, or a positive place? How can you program your subconscious mind for success?

The conscious mind is the boss mind; it makes the decisions; it's the programmer that programs the subconscious mind. Our subconscious mind is like a computer data-bank; it remembers, stores and retrieves information. It makes all your words and actions fit a pattern consistent with your self-concept—with your primary beliefs, values and attitudes. (It's vital to understand the relationship between your self-concept and your performance.) You can also control the flow of information that you put into the subconscious mind by recognizing the fact that the conscious mind can only hold one thought at a time. It can process these thoughts incredibly quickly, but it's only focused on one thought at a time. If you accept this to be true, and you focused only on positive thoughts ... guess what? There's no room for negative thoughts.

Since you can choose the very thoughts that you put into your subconscious mind, the most positive thought you can put there is your definition of self-esteem, and that is: "I like myself"—or "I love myself." The only things in the world that you have complete control over is your thoughts, your words, your goals and your actions. Positive, rather than negative thoughts, should eventually become the dominant thoughts in your lives. But remember, you're always free to change them. I said this before, but I'll say it again, because it's important: you should be programming thoughts into your computer that are consistent with the direction you want to go and the goals you want to achieve.

Blaming others looks to the past; responsibility looks to the future. The only part of human history you can control is the *NOW;* and the way you can control it is to control your **reaction** to a situation by saying, *I am responsible.* Saying *I am responsible* is a perfect example of a Positive Affirmation Statement; it reminds you that you're personally responsible for how you govern your behaviour.

Case in point: Let's say I'm minding my own business and someone comes up to me and, totally unprovoked, he starts calling me a bunch of names. I am responsible in this. I'm not saying it's my fault, but *I am responsible.* How? I'm responsible for how I *choose to react* to this negative situation. I owe it to myself to get out of it with a minimum amount of pain and discomfort, but I also want to be realistic. How I choose to react will have a direct bearing on what happens to me next. If I hit this person, and he's a very physical and aggressive person, he may hit me back. I may choose to walk away. He may choose to blame me and get angry, but it won't affect me because I'm responsible for my own responses and behaviour. I don't know how *he's* going to react, but realizing that *my* reaction will produce results, I need to force myself to consider all my options, so that I can choose the best one to reduce the impact of the situation. I have a choice here: I can either accept or reject my responsibility. By rejecting it though, it's like being cowardly; I'm saying I have no power-base, I have no options, I'm a **victim**. Or, I can look at the other side of the fence. I can say I'm the **victor**; I do have opportunities here; I do have options, and the more choices I can see in front of me, the more my personal power-base increases.

Remember that *accepting* responsibility is not optional. We *are* responsible, whether or not we choose to be. We can get angry or blame other people, but it doesn't change the fact that we're still responsible for *our own* responses, thoughts, actions and behaviour.

2. Key to Self-Management: Stress Management

This is your ability to cope with the ever-growing trend of having to do more with less resources. Stress management is funny in that you can't really manage stress, even though this expression, "stress management," is used all the time. Stress is not some green-eyed, long-tooth hairy monster that waits to pounce on us. Stress is nothing more than an internal reaction to an external event or situation. Chances are you have seen two different people experiencing the very same situation, yet reacting to the situation quite differently. One person is freaking out while the other person is looking at it quite calmly and saying, "Hey, what's the big deal?" What you need to do is not manage *stress*, but manage *yourself* more effectively and you'll actually endure fewer stress symptoms.

Stress can be described in three stages. The first stage is what I call "The Alarm Reaction Stage." This one can be also referred to as the flight-or-flee stage. In this stage, quite quickly, your subconscious mind interprets a dangerous signal and in turn triggers a whole bunch of neurological responses which ultimately trigger the adrenal gland. Now if you're going to fight your stressor, your oppressor, you have to be physically ready for the battle. But if you're going to flee, if you're going to run away from the stressor, you have to be ready to run a marathon.

This is how it works. Let's say one day you're walking across the street, then when you get halfway across you look over to one side and see a huge Mactruck barrelling down the street. Upon seeing this, your mind very quickly interprets a huge danger signal. It releases a whole bunch of adrenalin in your system, and you either lunge forward or jump backward to get out of the way of the oncoming truck. The other option, of course, is to stand still, take your best karate stand and say, "Okay, truck, I'm going to take you on!"

Well, obviously, that's not a very solid option. So when you come to the flight-or-flee decision in this particular stage of stress, you're going to choose to flee, to jump back. The truck races by you and barely misses you. As you realize that you're all right, you also realize that that was a close call, you feel your heart still racing, you feel your hands all sweaty, and a whole bunch of things are happening within your body. You've got butterflies in your stomach. All that is because your body has just gone through some rapid physiological changes in order to provide you with the coping mechanism to fight or flee.

A couple of minutes later, as you start to settle down and realize that you're okay, you feel the release of pent-up energy leave your body, and all of the energy dissipates. With this release you almost feel like (sigh) you need to have a little rest period. This is a good sign, because it means that all the energy that was building within your body to provide you with the energy you need to fight or flee has now dissipated. So it's not going to do you any harm.

The problem, though, is that in modern-day society it's not appropriate in some cases to fight or to flee. So we do a third thing. This third thing is called "suppression." If you suppress this bottled-up energy, over a period of time it will cause you problems. If you continue to suppress on a day-to-day basis you will move into the second stage of stress, and that's called the "Adaptation Stage."

The "Adaptation Stage" is actually when you're adapting to living under the symptoms of a high level of stress. You know you're in this stage when it takes you until the 12th day of your two-week holiday before you can finally unwind and enjoy yourself. Then suddenly you look at your watch and you say, "Holy gee! I've only got two more days left in my holiday." Your stress goes right up to the roof again. That's an example of someone who's living under too much stress.

Now, if you continue to spin faster and faster and faster what can happen is, because of your lifestyle, maybe your lack of exercise, maybe your eating habits and some other problems, your arteries may be shrinking and constricting the blood vessels within your body, and at the same time your heart is getting so excited because you're pumping faster and faster. Because you're under high levels of stress this can lead you to the third stage, which is called "Exhaustion." The "Exhaustion Stage" happens when you become physically and mentally exhausted to the point where you have a breakdown. Either a physical breakdown in the form of ulcers, heart attack or stroke, or a mental breakdown where you basically crack up because of the pressure of stress.

So the key thing in this whole issue called "Stress Management" is actually how to manage yourself with respect to stress. The most important thing is to keep the right perspective. What I mean by this is keep worry under control. One of the number one stressors in life, is that things can be blown out of perspective. Looking at a whole bunch of scenarios, you can say, "Ah, **what** if **this** happens, **what** if **that** happens?" Well, did you know that 40 percent of the things that you worry about on a day-to-day basis will never happen? An additional 30 percent of the things that you worry about on a day-to-day basis have already happened, and there's nothing you can do about it.

Another 12 percent of things that you worry about are concerns about your health. Now, this is not to say that you shouldn't be interested in maintaining a high level of health. Of course you should, but sometimes you get so preoccupied with your health and the health of other people that you can worry yourself to a state of being sick.

Another 10 percent of the things you worry about are what I call the petty, miscellaneous worries. These are all the big issues of life like "Who squeezed the toothpaste in the middle?" "Who stole my pen at the office?" "Who took my stapler?" "Who left the toilet seat up in the washroom? . . ." And all the hard-won silly little things that can get you so wrapped up in your life. At this point, a lot of people may be laughing because they can relate. But think of all the arguments you've had at the office, and all the problems you've had back at home, because you've lost perspective and put too much energy on the trivial unimportant issues that really aren't significant in your life.

Now, the last 8 percent of the things that we worry about are real, genuine worries. Unfortunately, half of them—four percent—are things that you have no control or power over whatsoever. So, either you have to live with them, or walk away from them. And sometimes in your own day-to-day working lives it becomes "sanity versus the paycheque." And that's what it boils down to.

On the flip side, the last four percent of the worries are important and you can influence them; these are the ones that you can spend the time and energy on.

So, my advice to you is if you're feeling a little stressed, don't worry, just take out a piece of paper and write down "My Worry List for Today." Write down all of your worries. Itemize them. Just by virtue of the fact that you're writing them down, you're forced to focus on your worries. And when you're done you'll say, "Hey, it's not that bad." All of a sudden, at the end of doing this exercise take your list and check off the vast majority of worries. Then getting down to a few worries, these are the ones on which you should be spending time on.

Even of the ones that you should address, you can ask yourself, "Of those that are still left on the list, which ones are likely to happen and, if they do happen, what's the worst possible outcome?" And once you can talk about the worst possible outcome, you'll say, "Well, even that's not so bad. So, why am I spending so much time worrying about it?"

3. Key to Self-Management: Time Management

Time management is the third issue of self-management that you need to look at very closely. I think it's impossible to manage time. It's like a person who says, "Well, I just saved two hours." How can you save two hours? What did you do? Did you throw it in the bank? It's impossible to save two hours.

I think what you can do is look at the 24 hours that you have each day, and say, "Okay, how can I manage myself with respect to time? How can I be more efficient within the given amount of time that I have? Either in a day, or for the rest of my life."

I think when you look at time that way, you can actually take the time and prioritize your most important issues. This is when you need to look at the rule of 80/20. This says, basically, that only 20 percent of all the things you have to look at on a day-to-day basis, are worth 80 percent of the importance of your jobs and your relationships and careers.

So, what you really need to do is spend 80 percent of your time on the 20 percent of the goals and responsibilities and specific actions that are going to give you an 80 percent return on our investment. I think one of the ways to do that is to clarify how you prioritize different tasks and activities during the day. This is a very simple time management system that is called the A-B-C-D-E method of prioritization. At the beginning of the day write down all the different tasks that you have to deal with that day; let's say you come up with 30 different tasks. Beside each of those tasks, write down an appropriate letter. If it is absolutely essential to complete the task today, you write down "A," because "A" stands for "absolutely," this must be done today. "B" stands for "it's beneficial." It would be beneficial, it would be nice to get this done, but it's not absolute. "C" stands for "convenient." It would be convenient to have this done, but it's not beneficial, and it's not absolute. "D" means it should be "delegated." It should be delegated for someone else to do. And "E" it should be "eliminated," it should be thrown in the garbage and never thought of again because it's a time waster.

Next, you go through and list all the different priorities for the day, the different tasks you have to do and you rank them according to their priority using the A-B-C-D-E ranking system. Then you set about taking care of all the "A's" first. And only when all the A's have been crossed off, do you move to the B's, and then to the C's. Tasks that can be delegated are assigned a "D" and all tasks that do not require any of your attention and should be eliminated get an "E." This forces you to focus on the 20 percent of the things that are going to make 80 percent difference in your life.

4. Key to Self-Management: Creative Problem Solver

The fourth key to self-management is to become a **creative problem solver**; to actually see problems as clever disguises for opportunities.

An average leader is confronted with numerous problems every day. When a problem occurs, the leader has two alternatives. He/she must determine if the problem is:

- not worth solving and forget about it
- worth some time and effort; then use the seven step guide to creative problem solving

The Seven Steps to Creative Problem Solving
Step 1: Define the Problem

A problem exists when there is a significant difference between what **is** happening and what **should** be happening.

Step 2: Decide on Its Worth

Problem analysis requires time and energy. A leader will find that some problems are not important enough to warrant any effort, and they should not devote resources to every problem that surfaces. The following guidelines can be used to determine whether or not a problem is worth solving:

- Does it adversely affect the employees' performances? Can significant amounts of money be saved; can quantity or quality of service be improved? The out-dated office decor may be considered a problem, but unless it affects performance, it should be given a low priority.
- Is there a significant payoff? Is there a large gap between the desired and the actual situation? Or is there a small gap that makes a big difference? You should be able to state exactly how the organization will benefit from the solution.
- Do you have the resources and the authority to deal with the problem, or at least make recommendations for dealing with it?
- Some cost is usually associated with solving a problem—are you sure that the benefits outweigh these costs?

Step 3: Find the Facts

Fact finding is conducted for two purposes: to gather data and to test data. You need to ask who, what, when, and where. These questions impose boundaries around the problem that help to discriminate between relevant and irrelevant information. To ensure the quality of information, there are three criteria that must be met:

- **Is it accurate?** Verify your information. Inaccurate data can lead to an incorrect decision.
- **Is it current?** Insist on current information.
- **Is it complete?** Gathering information costs money and has a point of diminishing return. You need a plan for gathering enough, but not too much, information.

Step 4: Identify Alternative Solutions

Once you have isolated a problem and found it worthy of your time and energy, you must then solve the problem. Arriving at a decision involves identifying alternative actions and choosing the one that will best yield the desired result. Experience also plays a role in making decisions. Most people solve problems each day by making simple, routine decisions. While these habitual solutions often work, you may be overlooking a viable, more effective alternative. This alternative solution could result in a higher level of performance.

Step 5: Specify Important Characteristics

Before you decide on a solution, you should have a clear picture of your ideal situation. One technique is to visualize the perfect solution and list its characteristics. For example, an ideal solution to a production problem would be one that is inexpensive, uses existing personnel, and does not decrease productivity.

You should list the characteristics for each possible alternative. Then, using the definitions below, you should categorize each characteristic.

- (A's) Absolute Characteristics—those that must be present for an alternative to be selected. If an alternative lacks absolute characteristics, eliminate it as a possibility.
- (B's) Beneficial Characteristics—though desirable, do not have the power of absolutely necessary characteristics.
- (C's) Convenient Characteristics—those that would be nice to have, like decorations on a cake, but they are not necessary. They would just make the solution more appealing.

Step 6: Weigh the Alternatives

Imagine that you are hiring a sales clerk. Review the sales clerk job description and assign weights (A, B, or C) to each specific task identified in the job description. For example: If you felt that greeting customers in a "friendly, open manner" was substantially more important than "filing," you might assign an "A" weight to greeting the customer and a "C" to the filing task.

Step 7: Implement the Decision

There are four steps you can take to increase the likelihood of a satisfactory solution.

1) List the difficulties this solution might encounter.
2) Make face-to-face contact with the people who are most affected by the decision.
   - Explain the need for the decision. This can help in motivating employees to carry out the decision.
   - Describe the goal. Knowing what the final results will look like can assist people in recognizing progress.
   - Involve employees in the plan. Employee's input into the decision-making process not only improves the quality of the decision, but can also increase staff's commitment to the decision.
   - Listen to any problems. Knowing the potential difficulties beforehand often helps you to prevent them.
3) Make certain the people who will implement the decision have adequate resources to do so, for example: time, money, equipment, skills, knowledge, authority, support, and most important of all, the right attitude.
4) Make sure the solution does not:
   - violate policy
   - interfere with previously established goals or priorities
   - cost more than it is worth
   - become so rigid that it does not allow any flexibility in its implementation

5. Key to Self-Management: Human Relations Skills

The fifth key to self-management is developing superior **human relation skills**. The most important aspect of maintaining superior human relations is the leaders' ability to communicate with their team.

Food for thought: *"All good leaders are great listeners."*

Effective Communication is:

- 7% Words
- 23% Tone of Voice
- 35% Facial Expression
- 35% Body Language

Effective leaders need to be aware of the seven most common barriers to communication:

1. Uncommon symbols or slang. Sometimes we have a tendency to overuse industry jargon. Do not assume that everyone understands what you are talking about.
2. Lack of communications training.
3. Environmental disturbances—excessive background noise or message overload.
4. Improper attitude, assumptions or personal biases.
5. Cultural, educational, or age differences between sender and receiver.
6. Sender/receiver relationship—employee/boss or parent/child relationship.
7. Speed of thought—the average adult processes words into sentences at approximately 500 words per minute, but can only speak 150 words per minute. The challenge is to stay focused on the meaning of the words and to discipline your mind from wandering.

Another powerful and quick reminder for winning human relations is what I call the rule of 70/30. This rule reminds us that when we are communicating with others we should limit our speaking to 30 percent of the conversation, thus we can listen 70 percent of the time. This is important because it is impossible to learn if we are not listening.

Three ways to improve overall effectiveness of communications:

1. Clarity—say exactly what you **mean**
2. Honesty—say how you **feel**
3. Directness—say what you **want**

Note: As the leader you are 100 percent responsible for both **sending** and **receiving** the communication.

A Good Listener	A Poor Listener
• Looks at the speaker	• Is inattentive; has wandering eyes and poor posture
• Does not interrupt	• Always interrupts
• Questions the speaker to clarify what was said	• Jumps to conclusions
• Shows concern by asking questions about speaker's feelings	• Finishes the speaker's sentences
• Keeps on the subject until the speaker has finished his or her thoughts	• Changes the subject
• Repeats some of the things speaker says to show interest	• Writes everything down
• Reacts responsively with a nod of the head, a smile or a frown	• Does not give any response
• Does not rush the speaker	• Is impatient
• Is poised and emotionally controlled	• Loses temper
• Pays close attention	• Fidgets nervously with pen or pencil or paper clips

Listening Questionnaire

Which of the following distract you in listening?

	Rarely	Sometimes	Usually
1. When there are interfering noises and movements.	☐	☐	☐
2. When the person is boring or has a poor delivery.	☐	☐	☐
3. When I am preoccupied with personal thoughts.	☐	☐	☐
4. When the person becomes too detailed in explaining.	☐	☐	☐
5. When I think I know what the person will say next.	☐	☐	☐
6. When the person speaks about something totally unfamiliar.	☐	☐	☐
7. When I get overly excited by what is being said.	☐	☐	☐
8. When I have a lot of work to do.	☐	☐	☐

Listening Questionnaire			
Which of the following do you do?	**Rarely**	**Sometimes**	**Usually**
1. Correct what a person says.	☐	☐	☐
2. Interrupt.	☐	☐	☐
3. Show impatience while the person is speaking.	☐	☐	☐
4. Get the speaker off the track by asking irrelevant questions.	☐	☐	☐
5. Try too hard to show you are listening, i.e., too many nods.	☐	☐	☐
6. Answer one question with another question.	☐	☐	☐
7. Try to get ahead of the story to guess the point.	☐	☐	☐
8. Give the person the feeling that she or he is wasting your time.	☐	☐	☐
9. Fidget with things.	☐	☐	☐
10. Fail to maintain eye contact with the speaker.	☐	☐	☐

How to Delegate Effectively

There are four characteristics of Effective Delegating. Leaders not only need to know how to inspire their followers, but they also have to share the work load.

1. Expectations and standards need to be very clearly defined.
2. Immediate resources are to be determined in advance, and made available to the person who has been delegated the task.
3. Priorities need to be established in advance.
4. A schedule outlining the deadlines should be established and benchmarks or checkpoints should be set.

The following is a six-step model to the successful delegation of assignments. After each step, I'll give an example from a retail establishment.

Step 1: Define the assignment, identify why it needs to be done. This step may not be necessary in all assignments, especially routine ones. Example: "Gary, I'd like you to create an attractive Mother's Day display in our front window."

Step 2: State your expectations of the completed assignment. Example: "The display should contain a cross-section of perfumes, books, and Mother's Day cards, et cetera."

Step 3: Ensure that the staff person has understood the action to be taken. Example: "We need to have this window display finished by 8:00 AM. Monday. Do you have any questions on what needs to be done?"

Step 4: Establish checkpoints and deadlines. Example: "I'll check with you at 11:00 AM. on Saturday to see how well you're doing and to make sure that you will be able to finish by 8:00 AM Monday."

Step 5: Troubleshoot for any possible problem areas. Example: "Are you uncertain what difficulties you might have with the display and how to deal with them?"

Step 6: Confirm the employee's understanding and acknowledge that he/she will complete the task by a set time: Example: "Okay, Gerry. You'll have the display ready by 8:00, right?"

Concluding Remarks on Becoming the Exceptional Leader

It is time to realize that we're living on a very small planet. Therefore we have to try harder; not limit ourselves to small dreams, but dream bigger. If you want to become the exceptional leader, you must: 1) accept yourself for who you are and what you can become; 2) give your 100 percent effort, best effort, in the application of all the principles in this chapter; 3) resolve to leave this world a better place than you have found it.

Remember, the world does not owe you anything; it was here first, long before you, and it will be here long after you. To be the exceptional leader you must know who you are, where you're going, why you are going and how to get there. Be the exceptional leader by taking the time to develop other people's leadership potential, and by leading other people, always by example.

Be the exceptional leader who leads for the good of other people, not for your own personal gratification and glory. Be the exceptional leader who knows how to lead by example and integrity, and *not* by practicing double standards. Be the exceptional leader who knows no discouragement and gives no justification and goes on trying until you've achieved your mission and helped everyone else achieve their personal goals along the way.

Be the exceptional leader who is willing to stand up and be counted; who, although the odds are against you, still stands. Be the exceptional leader who believes that leadership is an opportunity to serve your fellow person, to make this world a bigger, better, and brighter place in which to live.

Be the exceptional leader in a common crowd. Your service and contribution to your colleagues do make a great difference. Your family, your organization, your customers, and your country are counting on you to be the leader that you can become.

The final point on being the best you can in leadership is striving for 100 percent; one hundred percent of the best of your ability. Don't stop at 99.9 percent.

The following is what 99 percent quality could mean in a variety of situations in the U.S.:

- It could mean one hour of unsafe drinking water per month.
- It could mean two unsafe landings at O'Hare Airport every day.
- Sixteen thousand lost pieces of mail per hour.
- Twenty thousand incorrect drug prescriptions per year.
- Five hundred incorrect surgical operations performed each week.
- Fifteen newborn babies being dropped at birth by doctors each and every day.
- Twenty-two thousand cheques deducted from the wrong account each hour.
- Your heart failing to beat 32,000 times each year.

If your previous performance was at 50 percent and you're now at 90 percent, don't beat yourself up for not having the final 10 percent. Recognize and enjoy the fact that you're improving, but you must never be complacent about anything, about allowing yourself to perform at a level below 100 percent of your leadership potential.

A Short Course in Human Relations

The 6 most important words:
I admit I made a mistake

The 5 most important words:
You did a good job

The 4 most important words:
What is your opinion

The 3 most important words:
If you please

The 2 most important words:
Thank you

The 1 most important word:
We

The least important word:
I

Chapter Five

PERFORMANCE APPRAISALS

There has long been reluctance on the part of managers to appraise subordinates. However when performing the function of "manager" there should be no reluctance in measuring performance as accurately as we can. I find it difficult at times to comprehend the fear of "playing God" in a culture where individual performance has been assessed at least from the time a person enters kindergarten and throughout school and university life. In almost all kinds of group activities, whether in work or play, performance has long been rated in some fashion. Moreover, most people crave some feedback on how well they are doing. The controversy, misgivings and disillusionment that surround performance appraisals are not a result of people being measured, rather it is the result of how people are being measured. People can understandably take exception, resist or resent performance evaluations when they believe that they are being appraised inaccurately or against standards that are inappropriate, inadequate, or subjective:

This chapter on Performance Appraisals will focus on how to use performance evaluations as a method to assess the following managerial decisions;

1. Hiring decisions
2. Training and development decisions
3. Career path decisions

A Performance Appraisal is an evaluation of the employee's performance on the job. Performance Appraisals serve other functions as well.

1. Performance feedback allows the employee and the company to take appropriate steps to improve performance.

2. Appraisals help decision-makers determine who should receive pay raises. Many companies base pay increases and bonuses solely on merit, which is gauged primarily through Performance Appraisals.
3. Promotions, transfers, and demotions are usually based on past or anticipated performance. Often promotions are a reward for past performance.
4. Poor performance may indicate the need for retraining. Likewise, good performance may indicate untapped potential that could be further developed.
5. Performance Appraisals can guide career decisions, indicating which paths are most appropriate.
6. Poor performance may be symptomatic of an ill-conceived job design. Appraisals can help reveal such errors.

The value of Performance Appraisals can be illustrated by the following chart.

The Value of Performance Appraisals

R $\frac{1}{10}$ the value of Performance Appraisals comes from
E   identifying individual STRENGTHS
A
C $\frac{2}{10}$ the value of Performance Appraisals comes from
T   indentifying individual WEAKNESSES
I
V
E

P $\frac{3}{10}$ the value of Performance Appraisals comes from
R   building an individual PERFORMANCE IMPROVEMENT PLAN
O
   $\frac{4}{10}$ the value of Performance Appraisals comes from
           IMPROVING THE RELATIONSHIP

9 Cautions When Conducting Performance Appraisals

Factors that mislead when you are in the appraisal process must be avoided. An appraiser must be on guard against anything that distorts reality. Nine common pitfalls are:

1. Failure to provide each employee with an opportunity to prepare in advance of the Performance Appraisal interview.
2. Holding the employees responsible for factors beyond their control.
3. Relying on impressions rather than facts.
4. Personal bias or prejudice. Things you tend to react to that have nothing to do with the person's performance such as: race, religion, education, family background, age and/or sex.
5. Personality traits that have nothing to do with the job.
6. Judging those who are <u>like</u> themselves as better than people that are <u>dissimilar</u>.
7. Appraisers often rate all employees in the middle of the scale because doing so requires less effort and can be seen as "not going out on a limb."
8. Some supervisors are easy raters and others are tough raters.
9. Over-emphasis on favourable or unfavourable performance of one or two tasks which could lead to an unbalanced evaluation of the overall contribution.

Test Your Assessing of Others' Performance

Directions: Circle the number that best reflects where you fall on the scale. The higher the number, the more the characteristic reflects you. When you have finished, total the numbers circled in the space provided.

1.	I let the employee do most of the talking.	10 9 8 7 6 5 4 3 2 1
2.	I make an intense effort to listen to the employee's ideas.	10 9 8 7 6 5 4 3 2 1
3.	I am prepared to suggest solutions to problems and development needs but let the employee contribute first.	10 9 8 7 6 5 4 3 2 1
4.	My statements about performance are descriptive, not judgmental.	10 9 8 7 6 5 4 3 2 1
5.	I reinforce the positives in performance as well as seek ways to reduce the negatives.	10 9 8 7 6 5 4 3 2 1
6.	I try to support the employee's ideas rather than force my own.	10 9 8 7 6 5 4 3 2 1
7.	I invite alternatives rather than assume there is only one way to approach an issue.	10 9 8 7 6 5 4 3 2 1
8.	I use open-ended, reflective and direct questions to stimulate discussion.	10 9 8 7 6 5 4 3 2 1
9.	I am specific and descriptive when I express a concern about performance.	10 9 8 7 6 5 4 3 2 1
10.	My employees know I want them to succeed.	10 9 8 7 6 5 4 3 2 1
11.	I like being responsible for productivity.	10 9 8 7 6 5 4 3 2 1

12.	I like people and enjoy talking with them.	10 9 8 7 6 5 4 3 2 1
13.	I don't mind giving criticism of a constructive nature.	10 9 8 7 6 5 4 3 2 1
14.	I give praise freely when earned.	10 9 8 7 6 5 4 3 2 1
15.	I am not intimidated by workers who tell me what they really think.	10 9 8 7 6 5 4 3 2 1
16.	I seek and use new ideas whenever possible.	10 9 8 7 6 5 4 3 2 1
17.	I respect the knowledge and skills of the people who work for me.	10 9 8 7 6 5 4 3 2 1
18.	I follow up to be sure commitments, goals and standards are being met.	10 9 8 7 6 5 4 3 2 1
19.	I am sensitive to the needs and feelings of others.	10 9 8 7 6 5 4 3 2 1
20.	I am not worried by employees who know more about their work than I do.	10 9 8 7 6 5 4 3 2 1

TOTAL:_____

A score between 180 and 200 indicates you should be very successful in conducting Performance Appraisals. Scores between 140 and 179 indicate significant strengths plus a few improvement needs. A score between 100 and 139 reflects some strengths, but a significant number of problem areas as well. Scores below 100 call for a serious effort to improve in several categories. Make a special effort to grow in any area where you scored 6 or less regardless of your total score.

Source Crisp Publications

Let's Play Ball

Have you ever watched the individual members of a baseball team come together and jointly celebrate at the end of a game? There are many ways in which your job as manager is like that of a baseball coach. In order to win in baseball, your team must cross more players over home base than the other team. I see a lot of similarities between the game of baseball and the conducting of Performance Appraisals. The following diagram and explanations illustrate this point.

Overview of Performance Appraisals

Second Base One-on-One Communications

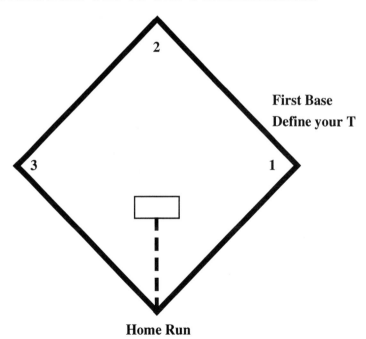

**First Base
Define your T**

Home Run

**Follow-up
Note: Cover All The Bases**

First Base: Set Your Target

One way in which the job of a manager is similar to that of a coach is in the motivating of each individual to meet high standards of performance so that together each person contributes towards the success of the team. Such motivation is possible only when you and your staff define and set a target of performance. The two elements involved in setting a target are **performance standards** and **performance measures**.

Performance Standards

Performance evaluation requires performance standards. They are the bench marks against which performance is measured. To be effective, they should relate to the desired results of each job. They can not be set arbitrarily. Knowledge of these standards is collected through job analysis and outlined in the job description.

Performance Measures

Performance evaluation also requires dependable performance measures. They are the ratings used to evaluate performance. To be useful, they must be easy to use, reliable, and report the critical behaviors that determine performance. For example, a telephone company supervisor must observe each operator's:

- Use of company procedures—staying calm, applying tariff rates for phone calls, and following company rules and regulations.
- Pleasant phone manners—speaking clearly and courteously.
- Call placement accuracy—placing operator-assisted calls accurately.

These observations can be made either directly or indirectly. Direct observation occurs when the rater can see the performance. Indirect observation occurs when the rater can only evaluate substitutes for actual performance. Indirect observations are normally less accurate because they evaluate substitutes for actual performance.

Another dimension of performance measures is whether they are objective or subjective. Objective performance measures are those indicators of job performance that are verifiable by others. Subjective performance measures are those ratings that are not verifiable by others. Usually, such measures are the rater's personal opinions. Whenever possible, managers should use objective, directly measurable standards of performance.

Second Base: **One-on-One Communications**

Even when managers use the most appropriate approach and the most valid method, the entire performance evaluation process can prove disastrous if the actual evaluation interview is conducted poorly. Many reasons can be given for this problem. The most prevalent include: the manager is not prepared or does not understand the important performance-related data for a particular subordinate; the manager is not properly trained to conduct a performance evaluation interview; or the manager does not do well in One-on-One Communications. As a result, the manager either offers undeserved praise, focuses too much on the negatives of the individual's performance rather than equally on the positives, or tries to finish the interview as quickly as possible.

Since describing the proper way to conduct an evaluation interview can take up an entire chapter, I have decided to offer an overview of the 5 steps to successful evaluation interviews.

5 Stages in the Evaluation Interview

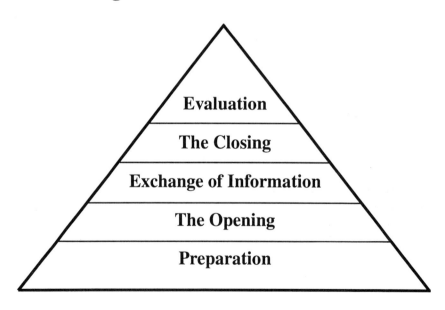

Preparing for the Evaluation Interview

There are at least three factors in a manager's preparation for an evaluation interview with an employee.

First, the manager should decide how often the appraisal will be. Most organizations choose either a standard review cycle, such as every twelve months, or an evaluation at "natural" points, such as the completion of a project.

Personally, I recommend that existing staff have a formal performance review every 6 months and the following review formula for new hires:

- end of day 1 (informal talk)
- end of week 1 (informal talk)
- end of week 2 (informal talk)
- end of month 1 (formal review)
- end of month 2 (informal talk)
- end of month 3 (formal review)
- every 6 months (formal review)

Note: Give constant informal feedback as situations dictate.

Second, the manager should spend some time and prepare for each subordinate's review. This entails gathering and reviewing all the important information and identifying the major points of discussion.

Third, the manager should set aside enough uninterrupted time for the interview to cover all the key points. This means that phone calls and visitors are held off until later. The employee must recognize that this is his/her time, not to be shared with other people.

The Opening

The opening is that period of time set aside at the beginning of the interview for the manager to put the appraisee at ease. By taking the time to help the employee get at ease, you will be reducing his/her level of stress. The more relaxed the appraisee is, the more likely it will be that the manager will get the results that he/she is looking for. You can help make staff feel welcome and comfortable by exercising typical social amenities such as: shaking hands, taking coats, offering coffee. The interviewer should always explain the procedure which will be followed during the performance appraisal interview. This serves to put the individual even more at ease by letting him/her know generally what is going to happen and about how long it will take. It will also reassure the individual that there will be an opportunity to ask questions towards the end of the interview.

Exchange of Information

The body of the interview is where the real communication takes place. Here, the interviewer fulfills his primary objective of dealing with these two key questions:

1. How well has the employee been performing since the last review?
2. Where does the employee develop from this point on?

Obviously, the way that the exchange of information is conducted is crucial. The interviewer needs to ask the appropriate questions, solicit pertinent responses, and report their rating of the employee's performance in a constructive manner.

The Closing

After you have discussed every necessary element, make sure that you close the interview with an agreement on what the present status of the work is, have a specific performance improvement plan spelled out and set a follow-up date.

Evaluation

Immediately following the interview, the manager should do at least three specific activities. First, the subordinate's file should be updated with all the information regarding the present period's performance. It may be useful for the manager to write a brief report that summarizes all the activities, including the discussion in the appraisal interview. Second, the manager should begin the next period's evaluation profile with a summary of the present report and any goals and/or plans for the period. Finally, in an informal way, the manager should let the employee know from time to time that he is interested in frequent progress reports on the person's performance, particularly if new data or changes are noted. The key point is not to appear nagging, but to let the employee be the one to initiate such informal progress reviews. In this manner, the two-way exchange of ideas and feelings has been enhanced and the relationship has been strengthened.

Guidelines for Effective Performance Appraisal Interviews

1. Emphasize positive aspects of employee performance.
2. Tell each employee that the evaluation session is to improve performance, not to discipline.
3. Conduct the performance review session in private with minimum interruptions.
4. Make criticisms specific, not general and vague.
5. Focus criticisms on performance, not personality characteristics.
6. Stay calm and do not argue with the person being evaluated.
7. Identify specific actions the employee can take to improve performance.
8. Set a time in advance of the meeting and explain its purpose.
9. Ask for and listen to the employee's evaluation of progress.
10. Emphasize the evaluator's willingness to assist the employee in improving performance.
11. End the evaluation session by stressing the positive aspects of the employee's performance.

Third Base: Setting the Performance Improvement Plan

A major difference between a highly effective manager and an adequate manager is the ability of the former to improve the performance of his or her employees. No manager who is truthful would say it's an easy job. It isn't. Ever-increasing paperwork, cut backs, global competition, unexpected crises on the job, and assembly line breakdowns all combine to make the job of improving the performance of your employees an easy one to put off until tomorrow or the next day. Yet the truly professional managers succeed because they don't put off the job. In fact, good managers see the task of improving employee performance as a challenge to be met, to be mastered, and to be used as a measure of their own performance. How do you meet this challenge? The best way to succeed in this area is to create an atmosphere of excellence.

4 Keys to Creating an Atmosphere of Excellence

1. Only the individual can motivate himself/herself
2. Catch staff doing something right
3. Treat them as team members, not slaves or children
4. Define high standards and ensure everyone understands them

Make sure that when creating a performance improvement plan that you include an action step for both yourself and your employee. Use it as a checklist to elicit confirmation from your employee of the steps that must be taken, why they're being taken, and what each step entails. Then make sure you write down, in your employee's presence, the completion date and expected result of each action step.

Home Run: Follow-up

Using our baseball analogy we have already reached third base by now, so all we have to do is cross home plate. We score a home run by following up the performance review process. Let's say that you meet with your employee at the specified follow-up date and find that his/her performance has not improved or has only improved marginally. What do you do now?

The first step for the manager is to be prepared. You have clearly defined in advance which disciplinary steps you will take if performance doesn't improve. We will discuss "Positive Discipline" further in Chapter Six of this book.

A Performance Appraisal Check List for Managers

The following check list is designed to guide the manager in preparing, conducting and following through on employee performance appraisal discussions.

I Personal Preparation

- ☐ I have reviewed mutually understood expectations with respect to job duties, projects, goals, standards, and any other pre-determined performance factors pertinent to this appraisal discussion.

- ☐ I have observed job performance measured against mutually understood expectations. In so doing, I have done my best to avoid such pitfalls as:
    - _____ Bias/prejudice
    - _____ The vagaries of memory
    - _____ Over-attention to some aspects of the job at the expense of others
    - _____ Being overly influenced by my own experience
    - _____ Trait evaluation rater than performance measurement

- ☐ I have reviewed the employee's background including:
    - _____ Skills
    - _____ Work experience
    - _____ Training

- ☐ I have determined the employee's performance strengths and areas in need of improvement and in so doing have:
    - _____ Accumulated specific, unbiased documentation that can be used to help communicate my position
    - _____ Limited myself to those critical points that are the most important
    - _____ Prepared a possible development plan in case the employee needs assistance in coming up with a suitable plan

- ☐ I have identified areas for concentration in setting goals and standards for the next appraisal period.

- ☐ I have given the employee advance notice of when the discussion will be held so that he/she can prepare.

- ☐ I have set aside an adequate block of uninterrupted time to permit a full and complete discussion.

II Conducting the Appraisal Discussion

- ❏ I plan to begin the discussion by creating a sincere, but open and friendly atmosphere. This includes:
  - _____ Reviewing the purpose of the discussion
  - _____ Making it clear that it is a joint discussion for the purpose of mutual problem-solving and goal setting
  - _____ Striving to put the employee at ease

- ❏ In the body of the discussion I intend to keep the focus on job performance and related factors. This includes:
  - _____ Discussing job requirements—employee strengths, accomplishments, improvement needs and evaluating results of performance against objectives set during previous reviews and discussions
  - _____ Being prepared to cite observations for each point I want to discuss
  - _____ Encouraging the employee to appraise his/her own performance
  - _____ Using open, reflective and directive questions to promote thought, understanding and problem solving

- ❏ I will encourage the employee to outline his/her personal plans for self-development before suggesting ideas of my own. In the process, I will:
  - _____ Try to get the employee to set personal growth and improvement targets
  - _____ Strive to reach agreement on appropriate development plans which detail what the employee intends to do, a timetable and support I am prepared to give

- ❏ I am prepared to discuss work assignments, projects and goals for the next appraisal period and will ask the employee to come prepared with suggestions.

III Closing the Discussion

☐ I will be prepared to make notes during the discussion for the purpose of summarizing agreements and follow-up. In closing, I will:

    ____ Summarize what has been discussed

    ____ Show enthusiasm for plans that have been made

    ____ Give the employee an opportunity to make additional suggestions

    ____ End on a positive, friendly, harmonious note

IV Post Appraisal Follow-Up

☐ As soon as the discussion is over, I will record the plans made, points requiring follow-up, the commitments I made, and provide a copy for the employee.

☐ I will also evaluate how I handled the discussion.

    ____ What I did well

    ____ What I could have done better

    ____ What I learned about the employee and his/her job

    ____ What I learned about myself and my job

Part of an Appraisal Interview

Henry Smith is a newly appointed district manager for Acme Electric Products Co., a manufacturer of electrical supplies such as light switches, wiring, fuses, etc. He was promoted to the position six months ago after serving as a salesman for the company for six years. He now supervises seven salespeople who are responsible for wide territories covering several hundred miles.

The semi-annual performance review of salesman Kelso Adams is due and Smith has scheduled a time for Adams to come to the office for the review.

1. Smith: It's good to see you Kelso. Come in and have a seat. It's certainly a lot cooler in here than it is outside today. This hot and rainy weather is enough to get you down. Has it been this bad out in your territory?
2. Adams: Yes, the weather has been uncomfortable. It's less humid up in the mountains, though, than it is down here.
3. Smith: Well, Kelso, you've had a long trip to get here. Perhaps we should get to the business I asked you to come here for—your regular performance review. By the way, did you fill out the performance appraisal form I sent you and bring it with you?
4. Adams: Yes I did. It's right here in my briefcase.
5. Smith: Let me have it, please, and I'll compare a few of the points to the ones I've made on the PA form I filled out about you.
6. Adams: This is the first time you and I have done this together, Henry.
7. Smith: Yes, that's true, though as you may know I've been a salesman myself for six years and have been reviewed every six months. But, Kelso, please don't hesitate to give me any ideas you have on our appraisal system as we go along.
8. Adams: Thank you. I'm glad to have any help you can give me and I can stand tough criticism. Just tell it like it is. I'm sure I'll learn from it.

9. Smith: I notice, Kelso, from your copy of the PA form, that we agree on many points. Here's one, though, that I'm unsure of. How many calls a day do you average on our A-class customers?
10. Adams: I think five or six.
11. Smith: Well, that's the goal we are shooting for. But when I analyzed your reports a week ago when preparing for this meeting I discovered that you're only making about half of the number each day. Is that right? And can you tell me why there is such a large difference?
12. Adams: I guess I didn't realize I was that far short. You know I have a very large territory. I travel about 45,000 miles a year, about 4,000 a month, normally with a couple of lesser months during the off season. So, I think it's harder for me to make five calls a day on customers than for most of your other salesmen.
13. Smith: Would it be helpful if we cut down the size of your territory to let you concentrate your efforts more?
14. Adams: That would save me a lot of travel time. But, it might also cut into my commissions with customers I'm building up. Look, Henry, I can cover the territory and get the customer calls up to the standard number again. It will just take a little better organizing on my part.
15. Smith: Fine, Kelso. Shall we just set a goal of five sales calls a day on A-class customers to be averaged between now and our next evaluation six months form now? Can we agree on that target?
16. Adams: That's okay with me. I'll get it up to that level right away. What's next?

Comments

Each of the following numbered comments correspond to the line numbers above.

Line 1   District sales manager Smith engages in small talk about the weather to lessen the tension of the situation and make the interview as relaxed as possible.

Line 3   Note that Smith had given Adams a copy of the performance appraisal form so that he could do some self-evaluation before they met.

Line 5   Most managers want to see the employee's self-appraisal before the meeting, to be better prepared.

Line 7   Smith reassures Adams on his qualifications and opens the door for him to suggest new ideas.

Line 9   While Smith knows that Adams doesn't meet the standard of five calls a day on A-class customers, he **asks** about them rather than taking an accusatory approach that might make Adams resentful and defensive.

Line 11 Smith corrects Adams but gives him a chance to explain.

Line 14 Smith's helpful attitude and suggestions to cut the travel cause Adams to resolve to get his calls up to standard. It's best when you can get the person being evaluated to make suggestions for improvement rather than you, in effect, giving orders to do so.

Line 15 An objective has been set and agreed to by both Smith and Adams. They have also set a deadline.

Employee Performance Evaluation
Instructions

I. **When Required:** Annual Review—to be conducted during employee's anniversary month.

New Employee—to be reviewed within 30–60 days but no later than 6 months after hiring.

Termination—A review will be prepared upon all terminated employees.

Other—when an employee performs in an exceptional manner, or when performance falls below standard.

II. **Who Will Prepare:** Employee's supervisor.

III. **Rating:**
- "E" 1. Excellent—Individual performs all tasks in an exceptional manner. Requires little or no supervision.
- "G" 2. Good—Individual performs many tasks well, and all other tasks adequately. Requires little or no supervision.
- "S" 3. Satisfactory—Individual performs all tasks satisfactorily. Requires normal supervision.
- "F" 4. Fair—Individual performs most tasks satisfactorily, but not all. Requires more than normal supervision.
- "U" 5. Unsatisfactory—Individual fails to perform many tasks. Requires close and constant supervision.

IV. **Overall Rating:** A summation, not necessarily the same as the individual's characteristics.

V. **General Comments:** This is critical. You must, in your own words, sum up the individual's strengths, weaknesses, and steps to be taken to improve upon those weak areas as well as potential for increased responsibility and job promotion.

VI. **Review:** By a person at least one level above the supervisor of the employee.

Employee Performance Evaluation

Name_____ Date_____

Dept._____ Job Title_____

Check one: ❑ Annual   ❑ New Employee   ❑ Termination   ❑ Other_____

Date of Last Review: _____ Date Employee Began Present Position: _____

Next Scheduled Review: _____

See rating information (Part III) on reverse side of this form.

	U	F	S	G	E	Comments
1. Job Understanding: Employee possesses a clear knowledge of the responsibilities and the task he/she must perform.						
2. Job Performance: The neatness, thoroughness and accuracy of employee's work.						
3. Job Productivity: The quality of the employee's work in terms of volume and accomplishments.						
4. Dependability: Can you rely upon this individual in terms of being on time and completion of tasks.						
5. Cooperation: The ability to work willingly with associates, subordinates, supervisors and others.						
6. Overall Rating						

7. General comments as to employee's strengths, weaknesses and action taken to improve job performance _____

_____

_____

_____

_____

Supervisor _____   Reviewing Officer _____

Date _____   Date _____

Has this report been discussed with employee?   ☐ Yes
                                                 ☐ No, if not why? _____

☐ If yes, note employee's comments _____

_____

_____ Date Reviewed with Employee _____

Employee's Signature

Employee Appraisal Form

Employee's Name_____Position/Job Title _____
Department_____Location _____
Supervisor's Name_____Date _____

Rating Scale

N NOT RATED—Insufficient time to evaluate, or the factor is not applicable to the employee's job.

1 NOT SATISFACTORY—Did not meet requirements or expectations. Fundamental improvement is required. Examples: Serious errors in work; volume of work is unacceptable or deadlines are missed; poor work relationships which hinder the work group.

2 ACCEPTABLE—Sometimes did not meet requirements or expectations, but performance has usually been adequate. Improvement could be made. Examples: occasional inaccuracies in work; sometimes volume of work does not meet expectations or deadlines are missed; work relations with some persons could be improved.

3 FULLY SATISFACTORY—Consistently meets requirements or expectations, without significant exceptions. Examples: Consistently produces accurate work; always produces the required volume of work or meets deadlines; effective work relationships with members of the work group.

4 SUPERIOR—Consistently met and often exceeded requirements or expectations. Such performance is achieved by a minority of employees. Examples: Work is always accurate and often surpasses standards or tolerances; frequently produces more than expected or ahead of schedule; work relations strengthen the work group.

5 OUTSTANDING—Consistently exceeded requirements or expectations. Such performance is a rare achievement. Examples: continued extraordinary accuracy in work; always produces an exceptional volume of work or completes work ahead of schedule; work relationships significantly contribute to the effectiveness and morale of the work group.

Confidential When Completed

Page 2

Using the rating factors which appear below, rate the employee's performance during the review period.

Rating Factors **Rating Scale**

OCCUPATIONAL KNOWLEDGE—
Concepts, practices and methods of the trade
or field.   N 1 2 3 4 5

QUALITY OF WORK—
Accuracy, completeness, thoroughness and
neatness of work.   N 1 2 3 4 5

QUALITY OF WORK—
Volume or amount of work; meeting deadlines.   N 1 2 3 4 5

WORK METHODS—
Following directives, regulations and procedures;
regard for safety measures; care of equipment,
tools and materials.   N 1 2 3 4 5

WORK RELATIONS—
Dealings with superiors and fellow workers,
including approach to teamwork, cooperativeness and courtesy.   N 1 2 3 4 5

COMMUNICATIONS—
Giving and receiving information; reading and
understanding instructions if applicable, writing
correspondence.   N 1 2 3 4 5

RESPONSIBILITY—
Initiative and reliability in performing duties; dependability in terms of punctuality and attendance.   N 1 2 3 4 5

FLEXIBILITY—
Adaptability to change in work assignments;
methods, procedures or conditions.   N 1 2 3 4 5

SUPERVISION—
(If applicable) Direction, motivation, development and evaluation of employees.   N 1 2 3 4 5

Rate the employee's overall performance during the review period. Provide substantiating comments for this rating and identify specific rating factors which significantly affected overall performance.

Overall Performance   N 1 2 3 4 5

Confidential When Completed

Page 3

Employee's comments on how well he/she thinks past objectives were met.
_____
_____
_____

Supervisor's comments on employee's specific strengths. _____
_____
_____

Supervisor's comments on employee's specific areas needing improvements. _____
_____
_____

Employee's own comments on overall appraisal. _____
_____
_____

Supervisor's comments on employee's promotional potential. _____
_____
_____

List at least four mutually agreed on objectives. Note: an objective should be 1—written, 2—understandable, 3—challenging, 4—achievable and 5— measurable.

1. _____
2. _____
3. _____
4. _____

Employee's comments on new objectives _____
_____
_____

Signature of Employee_____ Date _____
Appraiser's Signature_____ Date _____
Witness's Signature _____ Date _____

Confidential When Completed

Performance Appraisal Report*

Rating Code

Category	Rating	Descriptive Levels
Below Acceptable Performance	1	Performance well below that required for the position. Significant improvement in performance required to avoid termination.
	2	Performance is marginally below that required for the position. Frequently short of minimum job requirement. Should either demonstrate improved performance or be moved out of the program in a predetermined period of time.
Acceptable Performance	3	Performance acceptable but just meets minimum requirements. May indicate lack of experience in position or minor deficiency which can be corrected.
	4	Performance meets the requirement expected for position. This is the standard for acceptable performance.
	5	Performance exceeds acceptable requirements for position. Still requires some direction in handling complex or unpredictable problems.
Above Acceptable Performance	6	Performance more than acceptable in that it exceeds the requirement. Firm evidence available that acceptable performance could be expected in a more responsible position.
	7	Performance much more than acceptable and greatly exceeds requirement.

Section I: Personal Data

Name:_____Hire Date:_____

Job Title:_____Department:_____

Evaluation Period: From_____To _____

Section II: Performance Rate

Repeat the above steps for each critical requirement in turn.

1. **Performance Under Pressure**
    (Note: an employee Performing new tasks, or tasks with added responsibility, is under stress).

    Rating

    Below Acceptable: Was entirely ineffective under periods of stress/pressure, forcing others to assume some or all of his/her tasks.

    Acceptable: Maintained an acceptable level of effectiveness in spite of severe stress/pressure.

    Above Acceptable: Displayed unusual self-control in getting the job done, in spite of severe stress/pressure.

2. **Cooperation with Fellow Workers and Supervisors**

    Below Acceptable: Made no effort to work as a member of a team and greatly lowered group effectiveness.

    Acceptable: Made adequate effort to cooperate with others, and, by effectively working as a member of a team, contributed to the overall effectiveness of the group.

    Above Acceptable: Greatly increased group effectiveness by instilling a sense of teamwork into its members.

3. **Knowledge of Job**
    (Based on length of time in apprenticeship)

    Below Acceptable: Knowledge of job was inferior

PERFORMANCE APPRAISALS 169

Rating

Acceptable: Displayed knowledge appropriate for amount of theoretical training and on-the-job experience.

Above Acceptable: Displayed knowledge in excess of expectations, considering amount of theoretical training and on-the-job experience.

4. **Ability to Apply Knowledge**

Below Acceptable: Made frequent errors or was unreasonably slow in carrying out primary tasks.

Acceptable: Work was of an acceptable quality with few errors and with most jobs completed on time.

Above Acceptable: Both quality and quantity of work were superior. With human limits, deadlines were met with error-free performance.

5. **Adaptability**

Below Acceptable: Could not adapt to variations from normal procedure.

Acceptable: Adequately adapted to new tasks or situations.

Above Acceptable: Dealt with new problems and situations quickly and with minimum supervision, displaying imagination and flexibility of approach.

6. **Initiative**

Below Acceptable: Did not act when required action was obvious.

Acceptable: Took necessary action without serious delay.

Above Acceptable: Acted promptly to meet the requirements of any situation even though delay was possible.

7. **Responsibility**

Below Acceptable: Avoided accepting responsibility.

Acceptable: Accepted assigned responsibilities.

Rating

    Above Acceptable: Sought additional responsibilities beyond those assigned.

8. Complying with Company Rules and Policies

    Below Acceptable: Resisted company rules and policies.

    Acceptable: Complied with company rules and policies.

    Above Acceptable: In addition to complying with company rules and policies, suggested improvements to inappropriate company rules and policies.

9. Learning from Experience

    Below Acceptable: Refused to admit mistakes and rejected the opportunity to learn from experience.

    Acceptable: Acknowledged mistakes and utilized the opportunity to learn from experience.

    Above Acceptable: Readily admitted mistakes and actively sought the opportunity to learn from experience.

10. Punctuality and Absenteeism

    Below Acceptable: Punctuality and absenteeism record below the desired standard.

    Acceptable: Was usually punctual and was not absent from work without due cause.

    Above Acceptable: Was always punctual and never absent from work.

11. Productivity

    Below Acceptable: Quantity of work produced was below the normally expected, considering amount of theoretical training and on-the-job experience.

    Acceptable: Quantity of work produced was as normally expected, considering amount of theoretical training and on-the-job experience.

Rating

Above Acceptable: Quantity of work produced far exceeded that normally expected, considering amount of theoretical training and on-the-job experience.

12. **Capacity for Development**

Below Acceptable: Made no effort to develop potential.

Acceptable: Occasionally attempted to improve potential by positive action.

Above Acceptable: Was continually striving to improve value to the corporation by taking development action.

13. **Attitude Toward Job**

Below Acceptable: Needed constant supervision. Considerable time lost due to distractions or lack of interest.

Acceptable: Possessed an acceptable attitude toward the job.

Above Acceptable: Attitude toward job was such that it inspired others.

14. **Dependability**

Below Acceptable: Was not always dependable.

Acceptable: Frequently was dependable in all respects.

Above Acceptable: Was consistently dependable and inspired dependability in others.

15. **Commitment to Safety**

Below Acceptable: At times displayed disregard to safety practices.

Acceptable: Displayed acceptable standards for safety practices.

Above Acceptable: Constantly aware of good safety practices and made every effort to impact this attitude to others.

Total Point Rating   105

Section III Immediate Supervisors Comments
Training Profile

1. Is this employee, in your opinion, at a level of competence equivalent to his/her length of time in the apprenticeship program?
   Yes_____ No_____

2. What, if any, training do you suggest to improve this employee's effectiveness to ensure that he/she will become a competent tradesman/technician.

   1. _____
   2. _____
   3. _____

3. What does the employee being assessed see as his/her training needs? List.

   _____
   _____
   _____

4. What training has this employee completed since the last Performance Evaluation Report was submitted? Detail.

   _____
   _____

PERFORMANCE INTERVIEW DISCUSSION SUMMARY
   (include comments of person being assessed)

Immediate Supervisor's Comments: _____
_____

Employee's Comments: _____
_____
_____

Today's Date _____

Development and Performance Discussion Guide

Employee_____ Badge No.____ Cost Center ____

Job Title_____ Department _____

    This form serves as a guideline for employees and supervisors to jointly plan and review, on a semi-annual basis, the employee's commitments. Direct and open communication about all aspects of the employee's current job performance against specific goals, projects, and tasks is essential to make this discussion of mutual benefit. This form is intended for confidential use by employees and their respective supervisors/managers. Each will retain a copy of the form.

    Fill out the Job Accomplishments/Results Section first. The employee's previous performance is then reviewed and discussed. At this same discussion, future job commitments should be discussed and agreed upon. You will always be reviewing previous commitments and then planning for future ones.

    Remember, the only purpose of this form is to help the employee and the supervisor discuss:

- What the employee has done over the past 6 months
  (Job Accomplishments/Results)

- What the employee will do over the next 6 to 12 months
  (Job Commitments)

- What assistance and development the employee will need to accomplish his/her commitments
  (Job and Development Plan)

Review Date _____

Job Accomplishments/Results

(Review Period: 6 mos from _____ 19____ to _____ 19____)

Be sure to:

- Include any special projects or commitments added since the Job Commitment Section was completed.
- Where commitments are being exceeded or met (columns 4 or 5), highlight the positive factors which contributed to this success.
- Where commitments are not being met (column 6), describe the problem, the reasons for it, and alternative corrective actions.

No.	Accomplishments/Results and Discussion	3 Actual Completion Date	4 Exceeded Commitment	5 Met Commitment	6 Did Not Meet Commitment (see code)*	7 Commitment in Progress
1.						

PERFORMANCE APPRAISALS 175

No.	Accomplishments/Results and Discussion	3 Actual Completion Date	4 Exceeded Commitment	5 Met Commitment	6 Did Not Meet Commitment (see code)*	7 Commitment in Progress

* Code:

Employee did not meet Commitment, place one of the following numbers in this column:

1. Employee has the ability, but did not function adequately.
2. Knowledge or skill deficiency.
3. Unforeseen factors which changed priorities.
4. Other. Specify:

Job and Development Plan

CURRENT JOB: Identify below specific activities and resources needed in order to accomplish the commitments described in the previous section.

1. What will the immediate supervisor do to assist the employee?

   _____
   _____
   _____

2. What assistance will the employee need from other people or departments?

   _____
   _____
   _____

3. What will the employee do to ensure adequate knowledge and skill to accomplish the commitments for this period?

   _____
   _____
   _____

EMPLOYEE
DEVELOPMENT: What career related development will be accomplished during this period for the current job or future jobs?

   _____
   _____
   _____

Employee's Initials_____Supervisor's_____

Date_____

Job Commitments

(Planning Period: from_____19____to_____19____)
Next Review Date _____

No.	COMMITMENTS (including specific results and standards)	Relative Importance	Benchmark Date(s)	Completion Date
1.				

Comments on Strengths and Accomplishments

Identify the two or three most significant strengths and job accomplishments.

1. _____

2. _____

3. _____

Comments on Areas Requiring Development

Identify two or three areas where this employee needs to improve. (Set new goals.)

1. _____

2. _____

3. _____

Performance Assessment

Overall rating   (check one)

Outstanding ☐   Competent ☐   Marginal ☐

Previous Rating   Previous Rating By   Date of Previous Rating

_____   _____   _____

If there is a change in rating, state the major reason for the change:

_____

Employee Comments (Use additional paper, if necessary)

_____

_____

_____

# Performance Review and Communication

Prepared by _____ Date ___ Reviewed With Employee _____ Date _____

Manages the Job	Marginal	Competent	Outstanding
Recognizes problems			
Analyzes causes of problems			
Generates alternative approaches			
Sets realistic goals			
Establishes work priorities			
Organizes people and materials to reach goals			
Handles pressure			
Evaluates results			
Other:			
Examples of "MANAGES THE JOB" that describe your ratings:			

Gets the Job Done	Marginal	Competent	Outstanding
Initiates solutions			
Follows through			
Meets deadlines			
Achieves balance between work quality and quantity			
Takes responsibility for actions			
Other:			
Examples of "GETS THE JOB DONE" that describe your ratings:			

Knows the Job	Marginal	Competent	Outstanding
Demonstrates knowledge of job requirements, skills, procedures, techniques and principles			
Keeps current on changes in technical knowledge			
Expands knowledge of the job and how it relates to other jobs			
Other:			
Examples of "KNOWS THE JOB" that describe your ratings:			

Relates to People on the Job	Marginal	Competent	Outstanding
Acts as part of a team			
Practices 2-way communications			
Motivates others to accomplish their goals			
Other:			
Examples of "RELATES TO PEOPLE ON THE JOB" that describe your ratings:			

Performance Review

Name _____

Job Title _____

Date _____

Briefly list the major responsibilities for this position. Weigh each responsibility according to its importance.

Job Responsibilities—Rate the employee on each responsibility and give examples of the employee's performance (or lack of) that most accurately describe your rating.	**Weight %**	Marginal	Competent	Outstanding
(1)				
Examples:				
(2)				
Examples:				
(3)				
Examples:				
(4)				
Examples:				
(5)				
Examples:				

A Lighter Side to Employee Performance Appraisal

Performance Factor	Performance Degrees				
	Far Exceeds Requirements	Exceeds Requirements	Meets Requirements	Needs Improvement	Does Not Meet Minimum Requirements
Quality	Leaps tall buildings with a single bound.	Must take running start to leap over tall buildings.	Can only leap over short buildings with no spires.	Crashes into buildings when attempting to jump over them.	Cannot recognize buildings at all, much less jump them.
Timeliness	Is faster than a speeding bullet.	Is as fast as a speeding bullet.	Not quite as fast as a speeding bullet.	Would you believe a slow bullet.	Wounds self with bullets when attempting to shoot the gun.
Initiative	Is stronger than a locomotive.	Is stronger than a bull elephant.	Is stronger than a bull.	Shoots the bull.	Smells like a bull.
Adaptability	Walks on water.	Walks on water in emergencies.	Washes with water.	Drinks water.	Passes water in emergencies.
Communications	Talks with God.	Talks with the angels.	Talks to himself/herself.	Argues with himself/herself.	Loses those arguments.

Positive Discipline

The Beatings

Will Continue

Until Morale

Improves.

—Management

Chapter Six

CORRECTING PERFORMANCE PROBLEMS WITH POSITIVE DISCIPLINE

Joan Wright is in her mid 40's. She's a high school graduate, and is a single parent with two teenage children, a boy aged 16, and a girl, 18. She has been employed as a waitress at Island Park Restaurant for the past 6 years. Island Park is a family-owned restaurant which offers a fairly extensive menu, is licensed, and caters to a loyal following of noon-hour customers, as well as being recognized as an establishment that attracts an evening clientele which appreciates good food and good service. When Joan was hired, she satisfactorily met the requirement of the waiter/waitress job description. Over the years, she was regarded as a most competent and loyal employee. She was well-liked by customers and fellow employees. She possessed a pleasant, outgoing personality and could roll with the punches and in general, could be described as an exemplary worker.

However, during the past four months, the quality of her work has gradually deteriorated. At times, she seemed preoccupied and gave less attention to the details of her work. She reported late for work—15 minutes late—at least three times. On several occasions, she mixed up orders, and in addition, became impatient and curt with customers. She was also known to fly off the handle with fellow workers. The situation reached the point where during the past two weeks, four valued customers actually complained to management. If the difficulties are not soon resolved, the restaurant will suffer the loss of regular clients.

In the case study of Joan Wright, a key question that we need to ask ourselves is, "What is the main problem here?" Once we have identified the problem, we need to ask ourselves, "Is this problem a **training** issue or an **attitude** issue?" Take a couple of moments to decide before reading further in this chapter. Re-read the case and ask yourself, "What is the core problem here?" And, "Is it a training problem, or an attitude problem?"

I would suggest that it's an attitude problem. Joan has proven for many, many years now that she is an exemplary waitress, that she possesses all the skills and knowledge, and has a proven track record of doing the job well. Obviously she does not need more training. There appears to be an attitude problem here.

Now, with an attitude problem, when you're dealing with mature adults, what's the best way to deal with it? Unfortunately, many managers turn to punishment as a tool to deal with a problem. I believe that punishment doesn't work. I'm going to offer an alternative to punishment. A method that would work very well in this case is something called "Positive Discipline." As you can see with the first chart (below), there are four steps to Positive Discipline.

Step 1 is the *Oral Reminder*
Step 2 is the *Written Reminder*
Step 3 is the *Decision-Making Leave*
Step 4 is *Termination*

How does this apply to Joan's case? First of all, if you look at the next diagram called "Focusing on Performance Problems: The Interview Process," you can actually see the conversation that should take place between the manager and the employee in trying to resolve the deficient performance.

Focusing on Performance Problems

(The Interview Process)

You	The Other Person
1. State your CONCERN	
	2. Help the person identify the PROBLEM
	3. Help the person identify a SOLUTION
	4. Obtain a COMMITMENT on results
5. Restate your performance EXPECTATIONS	
6. Set a firm FOLLOW UP date and time	

These stages are explained in more detail on page 193.

Quick-Reference Checklist

Key Questions to Answer	Probe Questions
I. They're not doing what they should be doing. *I think I've got a training problem.*	
1. What is the performance discrepancy?	• Why do I think there is a training problem? • What is the difference between what is being done and what is supposed to be done? • What is the event that causes me to say that things aren't right? • Why am I dissatisfied?
2. Is it important?	• Why is the discrepancy important? (What is its cost?) • What would happen if I left the discrepancy alone. • Could doing something to resolve the discrepancy have any worthwhile result?
3. Is it a skill deficiency?	• Could the person do it if really required to do it? • Could the person do it if his/her life depended on it? • Are the person's present skills adequate for the desired performance?

Key Questions to Answer	Probe Questions
II. Yes. It is a skill deficiency. *They couldn't do it if their lives depended on it.*	
4. Could they do it in the past?	• Did the person once know how to perform as desired? • Has the person forgotten how to do what I want done?
5. Is the skill used often?	• How often is the skill or performance used? • Is there regular feedback on performance? • Exactly how does the person find out how well he or she is doing?
6. Is there a simpler solution?	• Can I change the job by providing some kind of job aid? • Can I store the needed information some way (in written instructions, checklists) other than in someone's head? • Can I show rather than train? • Would informal (such as on-the-job) training be sufficient?
7. Do they have what it takes?	• Could the person learn the job (is the individual trainable)? • Does this person have the physical and mental potential to perform as desired? • Is this person overqualified for the job?

Key Questions to Answer	Probe Question

III. It is not a skill deficiency.
They could do it if they wanted to.

8. Is desired performance punishing?	• What is the consequence of performing as desired? • Is it punishing to perform as expected? • Does the person perceive desired performance as being geared to penalties? • Would the person's world become a little dimmer if the desired performance were attained?
9. Is nonperformance rewarding?	• What is the result of doing it the present way instead of my way? • What does the person get out of the present performance in the way of reward, prestige, status, jollies? • Does the person get more attention for misbehaving than for behaving? • What event in the world supports (rewards) the present way of doing things? (Am I inadvertently rewarding irrelevant behavior while overlooking the crucial behaviours?) • Is this person "mentally inadequate," doing less so that there is less to worry about?

Key Questions to Answer	Probe Questions
	• Is this person physically inadequate, doing less because it is less tiring?
10. Does performing really matter to them?	• Does performing as desired matter to the performer? • Is there a favourable outcome for performing? • Is there an undesirable outcome for not performing? • Is there a source of satisfaction for performing? • Can the person take pride in this performance as an individual or as a member of a group? • Is there satisfaction of personal needs from the job?
11. Are there obstacles to performing?	• What prevents this person from performing? • Does the person know what is expected? • Does the person know when to do what is expected? • Are there conflicting demands on this person's time? • Does the person lack the authority? the time? the tools? • Are there restrictive policies, or a "right way of doing it," or a "way we've always done it" that ought to be changed?

CORRECTING PROBLEMS WITH POSITIVE DISCIPLINE 191

Key Questions to Answers	Probe Questions
	• Can I reduce interference by ... improving lighting? ... changing colors? ... increasing comfort? ... modifying the work ... position? ... reducing visual or auditory distractions? • Can I reduce "competition from the job"—phone calls, "brush fires," demands of less important but more immediate problems?

IV. **What I should not do?**

12. Which solution is best?
    - Have all the potential solutions been identified?
    - Does each solution address itself to one or more problems identified during the analysis (such as skill deficiency, absence of potential, incorrect rewards, punishing consequences, distracting obstacles)?
    - What is the cost of each potential solution?
    - Have the intangible (unmeasurable) costs been assessed?

Key Questions to Answer	Probe Questions
	• Which solution is most practical, feasible, and economical?
• Which solution will add most value (solve the largest part of the problem for the least effort)?
• Which remedy is likely to give the most result for the least effort?
• Which solution are we best equipped to try?
• Which remedy interests us most? (Or, on the other side of the coin, which remedy is most visible to those who must be pleased?)

CORRECTING PROBLEMS WITH POSITIVE DISCIPLINE 193

Looking at the diagram on page 186, the first stage says "You." The manager must **state your CONCERN**. How I would work this with Joan is I would call her into my office, very casually, very friendly, and say "Joan, can I talk to you for a second? Joan, there seems to be a little bit of a problem here. I've noticed that you've been late for work—three times—in the past short while. You've been short with customers. And also you've had some run-ins with fellow staff. Obviously this kind of behaviour cannot be allowed to continue. It has a negative impact on the restaurant, to the point where we've actually had some complaints from the clients. I'm a little concerned. You've been a phenomenal employee of this restaurant for many years. This behaviour is really unlike you. I'm just concerned. And I would like to know what's going on. Is there anything I can possibly do to help?"

You now want the onus to fall onto the shoulders of the employee. The second stage is where you want to **help the employee identify the PROBLEM**. The problem could come from four different possibilities:

1. It may indeed be a true attitude problem on the part of the individual. But it could be some other problem. For example, it could be that management is actually punishing positive performance.

    How does this happen? Any time employees perform very well in a company, their efforts are rewarded by punishing them—by giving them more work.

2. In contrast, poor performance may be rewarded. Meaning, that if someone doesn't do the job very well, some of the workload is taken away and given to somebody else. So, the good performer is being punished by being given more work, and the poor performer is rewarded by having some of the workload taken away.

3. Another thing that management may be doing is inadvertently contributing to the problem by sending out a signal that high performance isn't that important. Management might be very clear in how employees should act, but unfortunately they have failed to give these guidelines to the employees.

4. And lastly, management may have inadvertently placed some obstacles that become barriers to success for employees. One of the best ways to find out if this is the case is to ask the employee, "Have we put some sort of obstacle in front of you? Is there anything that is sort of policy, or something that management has done, that prevents you from providing the calibre of performance that we require of you?"

If none of those four issues comes to light, the thing that you're left with is that indeed, the employee has an attitude problem. So in the case of Joan, she needs to identify the problem. Maybe she'd respond, "Yeah, actually, there has been a problem. I've had a problem with my car, and also one of my children needs braces, and it's very expensive. So, I haven't had the money to fix the car and that's why I've been late because I've been having to rely on other people for transportation. I've been under a lot of stress because of the money issue. And I guess I've been kind of short with people."

Once the employee has actually identified the problem, move to the third step: **help the employee identify a SOLUTION.** As her boss, you might say, "Joan, I acknowledge that you said you've got a problem with the car and everything else, and I can certainly sympathize with your position. But now I'd like to know what can you do to fix it? I mean, where does the solution lie to this?" Give her an opportunity to think about it, and if she responds, "Well, actually I'm getting another paycheque tomorrow, and I can take $120 of that paycheque and use that towards fixing the car. And the rest of it I can put onto my VISA card and it will be no problem. Because then I can get the car fixed and you can count on me for being here at work on time."

Once the employee has come with up a solution, you want to ensure that she actually is committed to the solution and **COMMITTED to obtaining quality results**. Once you have received this commitment from the employee, then it's your turn to once again remind her or to **REINSTATE your performance expectations.**

You can do this by saying, "Joan, I'm glad we've had this conversation. I just wanted to remind you one more time that it's very important that you're here, like everyone else, on time, ready for work. And of course, we're in the customer service business here at the restaurant, so you've got to keep a very positive upbeat approach to the customers and to your co-workers. Otherwise you'll create a real problem for the business."

This would also be the opportune time to **set a firm FOLLOW-UP date and time** by saying something like, "I'm glad we had this conversation and why don't we meet back in two weeks from today, just to see how things are going. In the interim, if there's anything I can do to help out, please remember, my office door is always open, you know that. Just come on in, and say, 'I want to discuss this with you, or I need some advice, or whatever,' and I'd be delighted to help out. All right? Great."

This would complete the first phase of Positive Discipline. Basically what's happened here is Joan has been taken aside and had a very friendly

CORRECTING PROBLEMS WITH POSITIVE DISCIPLINE 195

chat and she's received an oral reminder. Let's say several days later Joan comes in once again late, but this time it's a half hour late. Now the tone changes a little bit. You move into **Step 2**: The *Written Reminder*. You would call the employee into your office and say, "Joan, we had a little chat three days ago about your tardiness and some of the other issues that we discussed, and I really have a problem. When we schedule staff to start at 9:00, we expect that everyone's going to be here ready to start working for 9:00. Not for 9:30. The problem is that everyone else has to double up and triple up on their work in order to make sure that things are ready for when we open up at 10:00 to meet that onslaught of customer traffic that's going to be coming in, and it's going to be busy right on until 2:00. So Joan, once again I want to reiterate my concern at how your behaviour is now starting to have a real negative impact on the workings of this restaurant."

Once again, as you go through the Positive Discipline interview, you want to get Joan involved in identifying the problem, coming up with a solution, and obtaining her commitment to the solution. Once you've gone through all that, and you've had a discussion, and she's now come up with some sort of solution to the problem, you need to reinstate your explanations once more, but this time take it a little bit further. You might say, "Well, look. As you know, we had this conversation three days ago. I'm now writing this down, so I'm going to actually document this discussion and mention that this is the second time that we've talked about it in three days, and we're going to treat this as a written warning. So it'll become part of your permanent employee file. And I'm only doing this to demonstrate to you the seriousness of this problem, and that it absolutely has to be rectified immediately because of the impact that it has on the business. Let's get back together Friday afternoon and discuss how things are coming along. Thank you very much for coming in, and we'll discuss this in four days on Friday afternoon."

Let's say about two hours later you notice that Joan is having a huge argument with one of the customers. So you quickly step in and calm things down a little bit, take care of the customer, and say, "Joan, I'd like you to go to my office immediately and wait for me, please. I'll be there in a couple of minutes." Then you soothe out the issue a little bit with the customer. You walk into your office and now you're into **Step Three**: *Decision-Making Leave*.

Let's assume the confrontation Joan had was a very serious confrontation with the customer. And it was totally inappropriate behaviour on Joan's part. And she certainly knows better. Well, in light of the flow of circumstances over the past couple of days, you should quickly state your concern that her behaviour has simply been inconsistent to what is required to operate a very successful operation; that her behaviour has been eroding the morale of the operation, has been impacting clients, and now we have a very dissatisfied client because of her direct actions. That being said, you walk her to the door and tell her that she's going to have the rest of the day off, with pay, and she's to go home and to give some very serious consideration to this important question: "Is she or is she not prepared to meet the expectations that are placed upon all employees of this establishment." Basically what I want her to do, is I don't want Joan to go home and to think about it. Be very clear and reiterate one more time what's expected of all staff at this particular restaurant. Explain that you want Joan to go home and think about that and come to the conclusion either "Yes," she is prepared to change her behaviour and accommodate you with this very simple and fair request. Or she'll make the conscious decision that she's not prepared to do that, and in doing so will quit her job. And if she decides to quit, her separation files will be ready for her early next week, including any outstanding pay owed to her, and any other documentation that is necessary. Basically, you want to give Joan the opportunity to immediately change her behaviour or to fire herself.

Now, if Joan decides, which most people would, and which is one of the beautiful parts of this technique, of dealing with behaviour problem and gives you a call and says,"No, Denis, I've given it some thought and I have decided to change my behaviour, and I want another chance to prove myself and my intentions, and I am indeed a good employee." Then you invite her back into the restaurant and she gets another chance.

But upon coming back into the restaurant, she's warned that she's run out of chances. That she simply has to comply with what is required of her. And she has to deliver at a certain level of performance or you will have to follow through with **Step 3**: *The Decision-Making Leave*. This is where you offer the employee to leave her job for awhile as her own decision. If she doesn't improve however she will be terminated from the job.

Step 4. One of the nice things about this whole strategy of Positive Discipline, is that it treats the employee as an adult. The aim is not to punish the employee, it's not to ridicule them, it's not to belittle them, or to hover over them like a condescending parent. Rather, what this is trying to do is say, "Look, the bottom line is, if there's going to be any kind of change of behaviour, a corresponding change in attitude has to happen." Management must reconize that they cannot change everyone's attitude. You try to make it easy for them, you try to show your staff how it's in their best interest to change their attitude, you try to be very supportive, and help out if you possibly can, but when push comes to shove, it's up to the individual. But keep this perspective very clear—it's up to the employee to change his/her own attitude and behaviour. It removes an awful lot of the attack mentality that management sometimes can't remove. And it also takes the focus off of the individual's *personality*. Rather the focus is on the problems with their *behaviour*. The nice thing about this approach is that there is no need for some sort of emotional argument.

There are 10 Specific Benefits of doing Positive Discipline.

1. **Early problem identification:** Since the supervisor does not have to reprimand the employee, he or she feels more comfortable dealing with the first occurrences of an issue rather than letting minor infractions slip by.

2. **Lower cost, less production disruption:** There is the cost of the one-day decision-making leave, but a traditional 3- to 5-day suspension means replacing the missing worker and disruption for a longer period of time. Also, the worker often returns hostile, even to the point of sabotage.

3. **Consistency of administration:** Since supervisors are more comfortable in the supportive setting, they are more likely to consistently apply the process.

4. **Reduction of grievances:** The employee has been paid for the day and is not likely to grieve the decision. Even terminated employees tend not to grieve the decision. Why? Because *they've* made the decision to leave.

5. **Applicable to all job levels:** A "Think it over" day works very well for hourly and salaried positions alike, including professional, managerial, and clerical jobs.

6. **Improved morale:** The employee returning from the paid decision-making leave has less reason to gripe and complain to save face.

7. **It enhances the organization's reputation:** The more fairly an organization treats its people, the better its reputation and its ability to attract and keep good employees.

8. **Removes the threat of human rights infringements:** Removal of punishment makes it easier for a supervisor to act whether the person is a member of a minority group or not.

9. **Improved employer-supervisor relationships:** Rather than being seen as a dispenser of punishment, the supervisor is viewed as a coach, mentor, and counsellor, and is often seen as being much more approachable and supportive.

10. **Employees do change:** It is common for employees to return from the decision-making leave with a new commitment to changing their behaviour. The returning employees may also have gained a new respect for the supervisor and for the company that allows the employees to make their own decisions.

In short, by treating employees as adults, and respecting the fact that they make the decision, management is more likely to reach the ultimate goal of having employees change their own negative behaviour. It's much better to take employees whom you've already hired and—supposedly— you hired for good reason, such as they were good at their job, and had a good track record—and help them turn themselves around, than to just say, "Oh, to heck with it, it's not worth it, let's fire them and get somebody else, because there's always another 10 more people waiting in the wing." The cost to hire new employees, train them, and go through all this process is too great.

As in many other personnel and management issues, legislation and regulation affect the discipline process and termination of employment. The following sections summarize significant legal implications and offer suggestions for avoiding liability.

Historically, America has conducted business under the Employment at Will doctrine. Simply stated, an employee can be discharged without notice for a good cause, bad cause, or no cause at all. Generally, an employer gives some reason for the discharge. This practice has led to a belief that explanation is required by law. However, the law states otherwise. "At will" means that the employer has the right to fire an employee without reason. Legislation such as the Civil Rights Act, the Age Discrimination in Employment Act and other changes in labour laws have eroded the "At will" doctrine.

Although employment "At will" was not questioned for decades, courts are now finding exceptions to the rule in wrongful discharge cases. In nearly two-thirds of the United States, state legislatures have passed new laws restricting discharge or discharged employees.

As an example, in 1987 suits for wrongful discharge increased 22 per cent in California, a trend-setting state on the issue. The damage awards in California cases for the last two years were in the $400,000-range. As a defense against wrongful discharge suits, employers must now clearly show that they have *just cause* for terminating employment. This change considerably affects employers. The improper termination of employment can expose an institution to significant financial liability. To avoid this pitfall, clearly document all the significant performance improvement discussions you have had with the employee. Keep accurate data during all performance reviews. Write a summary immediately after the discussion. Support your observation with the facts. Have the employee sign summaries of discussions. In general, make sure that you have ample cause when you discharge an employee. Written records will help protect you and support your word in a court case.

Equal Employment Opportunity Commission regulations are another legal area that affect disciplinary and discharge procedures. Their regulations make discrimination due to minority status, age, sex, and ethnic origin illegal. You can discharge an employee for just cause; however, even if that employee is protected under the EEOC law, as with all disciplinary actions and discharge procedures, protect yourself and your institution by documenting the causes. Also make sure you have not intentionally been biased against the individual.

Fairness Guidelines. A list of the guidelines that support just cause follows. These guidelines have aided employers in legal cases in which employees claimed wrongful discharge.

1. The discipline should be in line with the way management usually responds to similar incidents.
2. The employee should be adequately warned of the consequences of his or her alleged misconduct.
3. The rule that allegedly was violated should be reasonably related to the efficient and safe operation of the particular work environment.
4. Management must adequately investigate the matter before administering the discipline.
5. The investigation should produce substantial evidence of misconduct.
6. Rules, orders, or penalties should be applied even-handedly and without discrimination.
7. The penalty should be reasonably related to the misconduct and to the employee's past history.

EMPLOYEE WARNING RECORD

Employee's Name _____ Clock or Payroll No. _____ Dept. _____

Shift _____ Time _____ AM / PM   Date of Warning _____

WARNING

NATURE OF VIOLATION ↑
- ☐ Substandard Work
- ☐ Carelessness
- ☐ Conduct
- ☐ Disobedience
- ☐ Tardiness
- ☐ Attitude

Date of Violation _____

Time of Violation _____

Place Violation Occurred _____

COMPANY REMARKS

Form of Warning	WHEN WARNED and BY WHOM		
	1st Warning	2nd Warning	3rd Warning
Oral			
Written			

Has employee been warned previously? ☐ Yes ☐ No

EMPLOYEE'S REMARKS RE: VIOLATION

The absence of any statement on the part of the EMPLOYEE indicates his/her agreement with the report as stated.

I have entered my version of the matter above.

Employee's Signature _____ Date _____

ACTION TO BE TAKEN

Approved By _____ Title _____ Date _____
Name

Signature of person who prepared warning Title Date

Supervisor's Signature Date

I have read this warning and understand it.

Employee's Signature _____ Date _____

DISTRIBUTION OF COPIES

- ☐ Employee
- ☐ Foreman or Supervisor
- ☐ Personnel Department
- ☐ Plant Manager
- ☐ Employee's Union Rep.

The Twelve Commandments of De-hiring Staff

I think one of the most stressful things for anyone who deals with supervising or managing people, is firing a staff person.

Even in the case where someone has been caught stealing, or is insubordinate, it's still a difficult task. Because of all the emotions that come into play, it's just not a comfortable situation to be caught up in.

However, first and foremost, my obligation as a supervisor, manager or business owner goes to my other employees and their families, shareholders, partners and customers— not to some individual who, because of his/her actions, forced me into firing him or her.

I see the termination of staff as a last resort. I first try everything reasonable within my power to change a negative situation into a positive one; but for the good of the organization I must often bear down, bite the bullet and fire someone.

In my opinion, it's very important for your hiring/firing policy to be in writing, and should be given to all new staff at the point of hiring. One of the sad realities I see today, is that more and more employees who've been terminated are suing their former employers on the basis of *wrongful dismissal*.

1. Sound the Alarm

Assuming the offense was not so severe that it warrants immediate dismissal, in most cases of negative behaviour, *sound the alarm*. Give the employee a verbal warning first; second, a documented warning; third, termination. Giving an employee appropriate warnings can provide an opportunity for him/her to correct the negative behaviour. Point out to employees where they've been falling short of your expectations, what you expect of them, and that failure to comply with your expectations will lead to termination. If dismissal is inevitable, you have then established an excellent defense for a bona fide termination.

How can one determine whether an employee's problem is attitudinal or a training problem? A quick "test" you can use—*and I don't mean this in the literal sense*—is to imagine yourself pointing a gun at the head of your employees and telling them to go ahead and perform their tasks. If they immediately jump up and successfully complete the tasks, you know problem has been attitudinal. They can do the job, but have chosen not to.

On the other hand, if an employee looked at you with fear in his/her eyes and replied, "Gee, boss, I really would like to do that for you, but I just don't know how," you're confronted with a training problem. If this is the case, don't chastise the person; take the time to train him/her. However, if you've determined that this person isn't trainable and there's nothing else he or she can do within the organization, you'd probably have to let that person go.

Another area to look at is the corporate culture that has been created by your management team. A good question to ask your staff is, "What obstacles has management created that make it difficult for you to succeed in your job?" Sometimes the real problem lies not with the employee, but with you, the management team.

2. Take Your Time

Many people may take days, if not weeks, to hire the right applicant; yet people can make very irrational decisions and fire someone in the heat of the moment.

I like to try to give as much thought, time and energy to the firing decision as I did to the hiring decision.

Reminder: Make sure you've taken every reasonable alternative to change the negative behaviour, and that dismissing the person is the correct decision to make.

3. Don't Delegate the Job

If the person being dismissed works directly for you, the act of firing him/her is a responsibility you should never delegate. By doing so, this unpleasant task will likely be perceived as being unfair by all concerned.

4. The Timing and Location

Although I've often heard it said that the best time to dismiss someone is late on a Friday afternoon, I doubt if that is necessarily a preferred time, given the current flexibility in working shifts. Also, it can be anticipated that Friday is the time people are fired. I think it's better suited to when you can find a quiet place and a reasonable block of uninterrupted time.

5. Do your homework

This means being prepared in advance. Have with you all the appropriate records, forms, the employee's personnel file, and any evaluations you may need in order to justify your decision to dismiss this person. You should give the employee a detailed memo outlining the reasons for his/her termination, and include the final paycheck, separation sheets, and any other pertinent information such as accrued profit and pension plans, and the transfer of medical and life insurance.

6. Get to the Point

Once the meeting begins, don't drag it on—*get to the point*. The more you procrastinate on giving the bad news, the more difficult and uncomfortable it will be for both parties. Be tactful, be direct, be sincere, but do *get to the point*. One of the best ways to deal with initiating the conversation is, "Sally (or Frank), please sit down. These talks are never a pleasant task. It appears that things haven't been working out to our mutual satisfaction, so I'm going to have to ask you to leave the company."

7. Stick to Your Decision

The dismissal interview is not the time or place to second-guess your decision, nor to act as a counseling service for the employee. Your job is to convey the message that the person's employment is being terminated, and to do so in the quickest, most tactful manner.

8. Prepare Yourself for the Worst

The funny thing about human nature is that there's no accurate way to predict what someone is going to do in a stressful situation. So be prepared for the worst. I've seen very tall, robust men break down and cry. I've had women threaten me, while others simply stare into space and begin to mumble. The reality of getting fired can be quite a shock to a person. The key thing is to anticipate, in advance, the worst possible scenario. Chances are, it probably won't happen, but if it does, you should prepare for it. Always remember to act in a professional, courteous manner. Do your best to be sympathetic and understanding.

The best approach I've found, when someone reacts in a shocked manner, is to allow several moments to pass for the employee to absorb and accept the news, then try to move on. Re-focus that person's attention on getting his/her life back on track by saying such things as, "Frank, I certainly hope you'll find future employment that will be more in line with your personal requirements."

9. Be Consistent

If you give any form of support to someone leaving your organization, be consistent by giving the same type of support to everyone who leaves. There are three key types that can be included in a termination policy that you may want to consider:

A. *Financial help.* Above and beyond severance pay, you could include the continuation of medical and life insurance benefits.

B. *Secretarial support services.* Some companies routinely provide office space and secretarial support services for middle-line and upper level managers to assist them in their job search functions.

C. *Out-placement services.* Your firm can hire an independent company that specializes in helping displaced workers and executives find new employment.

10. Be Careful of How Your Employees Will Respond

It's very important that the morale of your organization doesn't suffer because of a dismissal. Whenever possible, it's important that you explain to your staff why the individual was fired, without being specific, and reassure them that their jobs aren't in jeopardy. If this goes unchecked, the rumor-mill can start working overtime, and you may have the entire staff second-guessing whether or not there will be any jobs for them.

Also, the person who has just been fired could be very good friends with many of these people and will probably still socialize with them, so it's important that you do what you can to stabilize the emotions of your staff.

11. Exit Interviews

Although these are generally conducted at the time an employee voluntarily leaves a company, in the case of dismissal you may want to conduct it in a few months following termination. These interviews help managers learn the employee's view of the organization. Some questions that can be asked are:

1. Were your job duties and responsibilities what you expected? If *No,* why not?

2. What is your frank and honest opinion of the following?
   - your previous job
   - working conditions
   - orientation to the job
   - training provided by the company
   - the pay you received
   - your company-provided benefits and services
   - your treatment by the manager

3. What could be done to make this company a better place to work?

   The nice thing about an exit interview is that perhaps there is some area of weakness you can correct in your organization, and minimize staff turnover.

12. Sum up and Learn from Your Mistakes

If you had to fire someone, chances are somebody made a hiring mistake. We know it's very expensive to hire someone, and an additional expense to fire them. To really get a handle on where things went wrong, you need to look back through the process, talk to other people performing that type of job, digest the information from the exit interview, and learn from this experience.

CONCLUSION

Now that you've read this book, keep referring to it as a constant source of practical information to ensure that you never have to pay the price of a demotivated or unproductive staff. Once you have the basic knowledge of proactive managing, the odds of being successful are in your favor.

I sincerely hope this book will help you be successful in your future endeavours of keeping your staff productive and happy.

Appendix I

Sample Compensation Policy

I. Introduction

It is important that each employee of Company ABC understands the company's compensation policies and procedures. The purpose of this document is to provide basic information about job evaluation, the salary structure and the administration of this Compensation Plan.

II. Compensation Objectives

ABC wants each employee to be paid compensation that:
- Rewards good performance.
- Fairly reflects the duties and responsibilities of each position.
- Is competitive in the marketplace.
- Will attract, motivate and retain competent people.
- Is internally equitable.
- Is cost effective for the company.
- Is a positive motivating force.

III. Job Description and Positive Evaluation

Each employee will have a completed and approved job description which will be used in the job evaluation process.

Also, each employee is required to review his/her job description annually with the immediate supervisor. The Human Resources Department should be advised whenever there are significant changes in responsibilities of a position so that a job evaluation review may be completed.

In determining the relative worth of one position to another, many factors are considered, such as:

- Frequency and types of business decisions made.
- Frequency and types of analytical and creative output expected of the position.
- Independent actions and decisions that directly impact the sales and profitability of the company.
- Frequency and importance of relationships with customers, suppliers, shareholders, the general public, government agencies and other ABC departments.
- Numbers and types of positions supervised directly and indirectly.
- The size and type of budgetary responsibilities.
- Special skills or knowledge required to perform a job.
- The minimum formal education required to perform a job in a satisfactory manner. The minimum experience required to perform a job in a satisfactory manner.

Note: Job evaluation is concerned with the content of a job and the evaluation into a salary grade—not with the performance of an individual in the job.

IV. Salary Ranges

Each job is assigned to a specific salary grade. Frequently, more than one job will be in a particular salary grade. Together, all salary grades comprise the company's salary structure. The salary grade represents the "going rate" in the marketplace for trained, experienced persons.

Each salary grade will have a minimum, mid-point and maximum salary for all positions in the grade. The minimum salary is a fair rate for a person who just meets the basic qualifications of a job, with little or no experience. The rate of pay for an experienced, fully qualified, competent employee performing all duties and responsibilities of the position in a completely satisfactory manner. The maximum of the salary range is the upper limit of potential dollar value of a position to ABC.

Each employee will be informed of his/her salary grade and the range for the grade.

V. Salary Surveys

To ensure that ABC salary ranges are competitive with companies of comparable size in similar businesses, ABC will participate in periodic salary surveys. The results of the surveys will be reviewed by the Human Resources Department and the officers of ABC. Salary ranges will be adjusted when necessary to remain competitive.

VI. Salary Administration

Job evaluation and salary structures deal with positions, their value to ABC and their assignment to a salary grade. Salary Administration involves managing and processing employee salaries. The policy of ABC is to base each employee's salary primarily on work performance—the business results that an individual achieves which contribute to the growth and profitability of the company.

Annually, the chief executive officer of ABC will approve a budget for merit salary increases, bases on recommendations by the Human Resources Department. Within departments, the size of employee's merit salary increase will be governed by:

- His/her performance on the job.
- Elapsed time since the last increase.
- The employee's current quartile in the salary range.
- The employee's recent salary history.
- The relationship of the employee's salary to his/her peer group within a department.

VII. Performance Measurements

Performance Standards

For each major responsibility of a position, performance standards will be established by each employee in cooperation with his/her supervisor, which describe when a specific position responsibility is being done in a satisfactory manner.

Business Goals

At the start of each business year, each incumbent of managerial and professional positions will also develop a few personal business goals, above the basic position responsibilities, which he/she commits to accomplish in a specific time period.

VIII. Performance Evaluation

At least annually the performance of each employee must be evaluated by the immediate supervisor and reviewed by the department head. Normally, this will be close to the anniversary date of the employee. Each employee will be given a performance rating from one of the following:

O. Outstanding

Optimum performance in meeting every basic position responsibility and individual business goals.

A person in this category has comprehensive knowledge about his/her field and is highly experienced. This person achieves significantly more in quantity and quality than other employees. He or she may bring exceptional creativity to the job. This person exercises rare business judgement and the performance usually shows a broad understanding of more than his/her own work.

An individual in this category represents outstanding performance in his/her position. This person requires minimal direction.

E. Excellent

This employee frequently exceeds the basic position requirements on some of the most difficult and complex parts of the job. He/she will also achieve some individual business goals in a timely manner.

This person requires less supervision than a person in the **G.** Good category. The individual frequently contributes a "little extra," anticipates problems and takes appropriate action.

G. Good

This employee is performing all basic position responsibilities in an acceptable manner. The performance is that expected of a qualified trained individual in the assigned position. Most work or projects are completed on schedule.

This person requires normal supervision and direction. However, the work of this individual probably requires more careful and frequent review than a person in a higher category.

M. Marginal

A person in this category is not performing some of the basic responsibilities of the position in a satisfactory manner, and also misses deadlines. This person may lack basic training and/or experience, which must be gained on the job.

Frequent and close supervision from the immediate supervisor is required and regular, careful reviews of the individual's work probably is necessary. With attention and application, the performance of a person in this category should rise to an acceptable level within a reasonable time frame.

A person in this category who does not improve to a **G.** Good level after a reasonable period, should be assigned to another less demanding position or terminated by the company.

U. Unsatisfactory

A person in this category, is failing to meet many basic position responsibilities and/or is particularly deficient in one or more of them. Frequently, this individual will need a disproportionate amount of guidance and direction from the supervisor.

Usually both the quality and quantity of the work are deficient and/or the person frequently misses deadlines.

A person in this category must be advised that his/her work is unsatisfactory and the reasons why. After counselling, a reasonable period should be established for prompt, significant improvement in job performance. If a satisfactory level is not reached after a probation period, the individual should be demoted or terminated.

Note: Generally, in a business organization, not more than 10–15 percent of employees can truly be noticed as outstanding performers and only 20–25 percent are really excellent. Usually, a majority of individuals should be classified as good performers in their jobs.

IX. Salary Administration

Merit Increases

The job performance of an employee should be the primary consideration in making a salary increase decision. However, other factors, such as the total merit budget for a department and the employee's position in the salary range will also influence the size of the increase.

Usually, an employee's salary will be reviewed once a year on his/her anniversary date. Normally, retroactive increases will not be granted. Increases will become effective on either the 15th or 31st day of the month following final approval of the increase.

A Personnel Action form must be prepared by the immediate supervisor and approved by the department head. The Human Resources Department must review and approve each proposed increase to insure consistency and compliance with ABC policies and procedures.

Promotional Increase Guidelines

A promotion results when an employee is given different and significantly larger job responsibilities that cause the position to be moved to a higher salary grade. (Note: an increase in the volume of the same work performed by an individual is not a promotion.) Depending on a variety of factors, a promotional increase may range up to 20 percent of the salary in the former position. Usually, the increase will become effective when the employee assumes the new responsibilities. However, sometimes an employee must spend an orientation or training period in the new position before he/she can perform the duties in an acceptable manner. In such cases, the promotional increase should be deferred until the orientation and training periods are completed. Normally a promotional increase should be large enough so that the new salary is at least at the minimum of the new salary grade.

Merit Progression Guidelines

Some positions are members of the job families, (e.g., Accountant I, II, III and Programmer I, II, III). Based on pre-established criteria developed between the head of a department and the Human Resources Department (such as education, experience, job skills, job knowledge, tenure in the position performance), the department head may advance an individual through the job family grade. An employee so advanced may be given a merit progression increase up to five percent.

Special Salary Adjustments

Usually, the salaries of new employees will be reviewed in less than one year or between three and six months for non-exempt personnel. Merit increases may be granted depending on performance and other appropriate factors, e.g., completion of the orientation and training period.

Salary Decreases

It is not the policy of ABC to decrease salaries except in extraordinary circumstances such as the demotion of an employee to a lower salary grade. However, even after a demotion, the salary will be decreased only if it exceeds the maximum of the new lower salary grade.

APPENDIX II

Detailed Trainer Evaluation

Rating scale:
Very High (5), High (4), Average (3), Below Average (2), Poor (1) & N.A.

1. Training Room Environment

A—Training Room Climate

1. I am effective in making the training room a friendly, happy place where courtesy, self-control and regard for others prevails. ____

2. I am effective in developing a quiet, thoughtful atmosphere in the training room and inspiring a willingness to work on the part of the learner. ____

3. By my actions in the training room, I show that I like my students and enjoy my work as a trainer. ____

4. I am successful in making each trainer feel that he/she is a worthwhile member of the group. ____

5. I remember that each learner is an individual who needs opportunities to express him/herself during group discussion. ____

6. I am constantly in search of ways in which all of my students may find several measures of success. ____

7. I am sensitive that an adult learner is often skeptical of his/her peers as well as that of the trainer and I am effective in setting the stage so that he/she receives approval. ____

B—Trainer/Learner Relationships

1. In my relationships with students, I am:
    a. courteous _____
    b. tactful _____
    c. flexible _____
    d. empathetic _____
    e. sympathetic _____
    f. frank and honest _____
    g. open-minded _____
    h. cheerful and optimistic _____
    i. fair _____
    j. relaxed and at ease _____
    k. enthusiastic _____
    l. consistent _____

2. I am concerned with the welfare of my students _____
3. I am alert and responsive to the needs and concerns of my students _____
4. I am willing to admit that I have made an error _____
5. I commend effort and give praise to work well done _____
6. My students appear to feel secure and satisfied _____
7. I provide time and physical arrangements to allow students their own space _____
8. The openness of communications in my training room is _____
9. The degree to which I demonstrate my interest in and support for student initiated activity is _____
10. I encourage students to work to their potential _____

11. I encourage student self-discipline ___
12. I encourage learning through cooperation ___
13. The development of self-reliance among my students is ___
14. The extent to which I am a good listener is ___
15. My encouragement of student creativity, exploration is ___
16. I treat all my students equally ___
17. The degree to which I believe my relationship with my students is based on trust and respect is ___
18. My skill at dealing with particular physical and learning disabilities in my students is ___
19. My responsiveness to individual differences is ___
20. The extent to which I foster in my students:
    a. a respect for others is ___
    b. a respect for the property of others is ___
    c. the importance of peace and goodwill is ___
    d. a sharing attitude is ___

C—Management

Good management entails trainer and students working harmoniously together, with continuous growth on the part of the learners towards inhancing their personal and professional skills.

1. Because curriculum is carefully prepared and well organized, my students have confidence that I know what I am doing, and management difficulties are minimal. ___
2. I keep my students busy at interesting and useful projects/case studies. ___
3. In assigning work:

   I expect and wait for complete learner attention. ___
   I make sure my students know what to do. ___
   I keep my talking to a minimum. ___

4. I have a calm and sensible outlook on my work and avoid shouting and displaying a hostile attitude. ___
5. I maintain consistent expectations of student behaviour. ___
6. I make clear to the class my standards of student behaviour. ___
7. I make clear to the class objectives and procedures for evaluating. ___
8. I encourage self-discipline. ___
9. I cope with training disruptions in a positive manner. ___

2. Techniques and Methods

A—Program

1. I make use of an integrated program so that each skill area receives a fair degree of emphasis. ___
2. I give careful thought to the needs and interests of my students and together with them plan for meaningful learning experiences. ___
3. My visuals and handwork are prepared in advance. ___
4. I use training supplies and materials to their potential. ___
5. By frequent use of thoughtful questions, learning experiences, illustrations, etc., I am effective in stimulating learner interest. ___
6. All my students participate in class discussions, thought-provoking seatwork, or other activities, following each session. ___
7. I make provisions for differences in ability, experience and outlook among my students, so that some measure of success is possible for every learner. ___
8. I provide opportunities for learner to develop the ability to work effectively in groups, as well as individually. ___
9. I am thoroughly acquainted with the internal and external resources which can assist me in my training. ___
10. I create and maintain appropriate intellectual and emotional climates for learning. ___

11. I present lessons so that they are clearly understood. ___
12. I sequence questions to lead students to higher levels of thinking. ___
13. I capitalize on pertinent student questions. ___
14. I lead students to self-discovery of principles, generalizations and concepts. ___
15. I foster a thoughtful, questioning attitude. ___
16. I provide an appropriate mix between trainer/presenter and student participation in my lessons. ___

B—Evaluating

1. My evaluation program is:
    a. in keeping with the stated objectives of the organization. ___
    b. in keeping with the stated objectives of the program. ___
    c. consistent with that of my colleagues. ___
    d. consistent with adult learning principles. ___
2. I use a variety of standardized achievement and diagnostic tests and trainer-made objective and subjective tests. ___
3. My evaluation program makes provision for testing:
    a. skills ___
    b. knowledge of content ___
    c. concepts ___
    d. generalization ___
    e. applications ___
    f. reasoning ___
4. I use evaluation results to:
    a. analyze effectiveness of training ___
    b. plan instruction and reviews ___
    c. diagnose strengths and weaknesses of the individual student ___

    d. implement strategies to meet the needs as diagnosed ____

5. I keep accurate and complete records with respect to:

    a. attendance ____

    b. achievement ____

3. Personal Attributes

A—Personal Qualities

1. I am enthusiastic and sincere about my work, and pleasant and patient with my students. ____
2. I show interest in each individual. ____
3. I demonstrate warmth, friendliness and a sense of humour and understanding. ____
4. I demonstrate enthusiasm for the profession. ____
5. I am well-spoken and concise; my voice is relaxed, clear, pleasant and not too loud. ____
6. I demonstrate good grooming and habits of dress. ____
7. I show by my actions that I have a good measure of common sense. ____
8. I model good work habits which reflect punctuality, dependability, efficiency and accuracy. ____

B—Staff Relations

1. I am willing and cheerful and strive to work harmoniously with the departments of the organization. ____
2. I am open to suggestion for improvement and show initiative in using new ideas. ____
3. I treat each staff member with respect and dignity. ____
4. I make a special effort to make welcome and offer assistance to new trainers. ____
5. I maintain a good working relationship with all program personnel. ____
6. I refrain from criticizing the organization or employees in public. ____

7. I actively participate by speaking up at staff meetings. ___
8. I understand the relationship of my subject area to the others within the context of the total organization. ___

4. Professional Attributes

A—Professional Growth

1. I participate in conferences and workshops to improve instruction. ___
2. I read professional materials. ___
3. I work with colleagues to improve curriculum and instructional techniques. ___
4. I work with colleagues to enhance the status of the profession. ___
5. I participate in educational organizations. ___
6. I enhance my academic development through continued formal education activities. ___
7. I am involved in professional associations (ASTD), (NSA), (MPI) . . . ___

B—Knowledge

1. I am academically content in the area of my training assignment. ___
2. I am knowlegeable of adult learning theories. ___
3. I am knowledgeable of adult psychology. ___
4. I am familiar with techniques of curriculum development. ___
5. I am knowledgeable about current research findings in my area of training. ___
6. I am aware of new methodology. ___
7. I am aware of the policies of the organization. ___
8. I am aware of trainer rights, duties and legal responsibilities ___

APPENDIX III

- Equal Employment Opportunity Commission Offices
- State Fair Employment Practicies Offices
- Books
- Current Periodicals

Equal Employment Opportunity Commission Offices

Administrative Offices
2401 E. Street, N.W.
Washington, D.C. 20507 U.S.A.
(202) 634-6922
(800) USA-EEOC

Albuquerque Area Office
(Phoenix District)
Western Bank Bldg., Suite 1105
505 Marquette, N.W.
Albuquerque, NM 87101 U.S.A.
(505) 766-2061

Atlanta District Office
Citizens Trust Building
75 Piedmont Ave., N.W. Suite 1100
Atlanta, GA 30335 U.S.A.
(404) 331-6091

Chicago District Office
Federal Building, Room 930-A
536 South Clark Street
Chicago, IL 60605 U.S.A.
(312) 353-2713

Cincinnati Area Office
(Cleveland District)
Federal Building, Room 7015
550 Main Street
Cincinnati, OH 44115 U.S.A.
(513) 684-2851

Cleveland District Office
1375 Euclid Avenue, Room 600
Cleveland OH 44115 U.S.A.
(216) 522-7425

Baltimore District Office
109 Market Place, Suite 4000
Baltimore, MD 21202 U.S.A.
(301) 962-3932

Birmingham District Office
2121 Eighth Avenue, North
Suite 824
Birmingham, AL 35203 U.S.A.
(205) 254-0082

Boston Area Office
(New York District)
JFK Building, Room 409-B
Boston, MA 02203 U.S.A.
(617) 223-4535

Buffalo Local Office
(New York District)
Guaranty Building
28 Church Street
Buffalo, NY 14202 U.S.A.
(716) 846-4441

Charlotte District Office
5500 Central Avenue
Charlotte, NC 28212 U.S.A.
(704) 567-7100

Fresno Area Office
(San Francisco District)
1313 P Street, Suite 103
Fresno, CA 93721 U.S.A.
(209) 487-5793

Dallas District Office
8303 Elmbrook Drive
Dallas, TX 75247 U.S.A.
(214) 767-7015

Dayton Area Office
(Cleveland District)
Federal Building
200 W. Second Street, Room 608
Dayton, OH 45402 U.S.A.
(513) 225-2753

Denver District Office
1845 Sheman Street, 2nd. Floor
Denver, CO, 80203 U.S.A.
(303) 837-2771

Detroit District Office
Patrick V. MacNamara Federal Bldg
477 Michigan Avenue, Room 1540
Detroit, MI 48226 U.S.A.
(313) 226-7636

El Paso Office
(Dallas District)
First National Bldg., Ste. 1112
109 North Oregon Street
El Paso, TX 79901 U.S.A.
(915) 541-7596

Louisville Area Office
(Memphis District)
601 West Broadway, Room 104
Louisville, KY 40202 U.S.A.
(502) 582-6082

Greensboro Local Office
(Charlotte District)
324 W. Market St., Room B-27
Post Office Box 3363
Greensboro, NC 27402 U.S.A.
(919) 333-5174

Greenville Local Office
(Atlanta District)
Century Plaza, Suite 109-B
211 Century Drive
Greenville, SC 29607 U.S.A.
(803) 233-1791

Houston District Office
405 Main Street, Sixth Floor
Houston, TX 77002 U.S.A.
(713) 226-2601

Indianapolis District Office
Federal Bldg., U.S. Courthouse
46 E. Ohio Street, Room 456
Indianapolis, IN 46204 U.S.A.
(317) 269-7212

Jackson Area Office
(Birmingham District)
McCoy Federal Office Building
100 W. Capitol St., Suite 721
Jackson, MS 39269 U.S.A.
(601) 965-4537

Kansas Area Office
(St. Louis District)
911 Walnut, 10th. Floor
Kanas City, MO 94106 U.S.A.
(816) 374-5773

Memphis District Office
1407 Union Avenue, Suite 502
Memphis, TN 38104 U.S.A.
(901) 521-2617

Miami District Office
Metro Mall
1 Northeast First St., 6th. Fl.
Miami, FL 33132 U.S.A.
(305) 536-4491

Milwaukee District Office
310 W. Wisconsin Ave.
Suite 800
Milwaukee, WI 53203 U.S.A.
(414) 291-1111

Minneapolis Local Office
(Milwaukee District)
110 S. Fourth St., Room 17
Minneapolis, MN 55401 U.S.A.
(612) 349-3495

Nashville Area Office
(Memphis District)
Parkway Towers, Suite 1100
Nashville, TN 37219 U.S.A.
(615) 251-5820

Newark Area Office
(New York District)
60 Park Place, Room 301
Newark, NJ 07102 U.S.A.
(201) 645-6383

Little Rock Area Office
(New Orleans District)
Savers Building, Suite 621
320 West Capitol Avenue
Little Rock, AR 72201 U.S.A.
(501) 378-5060

Los Angeles District Office
3660 Wilshire Blvd., 5th. Floor
Los Angeles, CA 90010 U.S.A.
(213) 251-7278

Oakland Local Office
(San Francisco District)
Wells Fargo Bank Building
1333 Broadway, Room 430
Oakland, CA 94612   U.S.A.
(415) 273-7588

Oklahoma Area Office
(Dallas District)
Alfred P. Marrah Federal Bldg.
200 N.W. Fifth St., Room 703
Oklahoma City, OK 73102 U.S.A.
(405) 231-4911

Philadelphia District Office
127 North 4th. St., Suite 300
Philadelphia, PA 19106 U.S.A.
(215) 597-7784

New Orleans District Office
F. Edward Hebert Federal Bldg.
600 S. Maestri Place, Room 528
New Orleans, LA 70130 U.S.A.
(504) 589-2329

New York District Office
90 Church Street, Room 1505
New York, NY 10007 U.S.A.
(212) 264-7161

Norfolk Area Office
(Baltimore District)
Federal Building, Room 412
200 Granby Mall
Norfolk, VA 23510 U.S.A.
(804) 441-3470

San Francisco District Office
10 United Nations Plaza
Fourth Floor
San Francisco, CA 94102 U.S.A.
(415) 556-0260

San Jose Local Office
(San Francisco District)
U.S. Courthouse & Fed. Bldg.
280 S First Street, Room 4150
San Jose, CA 95113 U.S.A.
(408) 291-7352

Phoenix District Office
135 N. Second Ave., 5th. Floor
Phoenix, AZ 85003 U.S.A.
(602) 261-3882

Pittsburg Area Office
(Philadelphia District)
Federal Building, Rm. 2038A
1000 Liberty Avenue
Pittsburg, PA 15222 U.S.A.
(412) 644-3444

Raleigh Area Office
(Charlotte District)
178 W. Hargett St., Suite 500
Raleigh, NC 27601 U.S.A.
(919) 856-4064

Richmond Area Office
(Baltimore District)
400 N. 8th. St., Room 6206
Richmond, VA 23240 U.S.A.
(804) 771-2692

San Antonio Area Office
(Houston District)
727 East Durango, Suite 601-B
San Antonio, TX 78206 U.S.A.
(515) 229-6051

Seattle District Office
Arcade Plaza Building
1321 Second Ave., 7th. Floor
Seattle, WA 98101 U.S.A.
(206) 442-0968

St. Louis District Office
625 N. Euclid Street
St. Louis, MO 63108 U.S.A.
(314) 425-6585

Tampa Area Office
(Miami District)
700 Twiggs Street, Room 302
Tampa, FL 33602 U.S.A.
(813) 228-2310

Washington Area Office
(Baltimore District)
1717 H. St., N.W., Suite 400
Washington, DC 20006 U.S.A.
(202) 653-6197

San Diego Local Office
(Los Angeles District)
San Diego Federal Building
880 Front Street
San Diego, CA 92188 U.S.A.
(619) 293-6288

State Fair Employment Practice Offices

ALASKA
State Commission for Human Rights
431 W. 7th. Ave., Ste. 101
Anchorage, AK 99501
U.S.A.
(907) 276-7474

ARIZONA
Civil Rights Division
Attorney General's Office
1275 W. Washington St.
Phoenix, AZ 85007
U.S.A.
(602) 255-5263

CALIFORNIA
Department of Fair Employment
and Housing
1201 I Street, Suite 211
Sacramento, CA 95814
U.S.A.
(916) 445-9918

COLORADO
Civil Rights Commission
Room 600C State Services Bldg.,
1525 Sherman Street
Denver, CO 80203
U.S.A.
(303) 866-2621

GEORGIA
Georgia Office of Fair Employment
Practices
156 Trinity Ave., S.W.,
Suite 208
Atlanta, GA 30303
U.S.A.

HAWAII
Department of Labour and
Industrial Relations
888 Mililani St. Room 401
Honolulu, HI 96813
U.S.A.
(808) 548-3976

IDAHO
Commission on Human Rights
450 W. State Street
Boise, ID 83720
U.S.A.
(208) 334-2873

ILLINOIS
Department Of Human Rights
One Illinois Center
100 W. Randolph St., Suite 10-100
Chicago, IL 60601
U.S.A.
(312) 917-6200

CONNECTICUT
Commission on Human Rights and
Opportunities
90 Washington Street
Hartford, CT 06115
U.S.A.
(203) 566-3350

DELAWARE
Department of Labour
Anti-Discrimination Section
Wilmington State Office Bldg.
820 N. French St., 6th. Floor
Wilmington, DE 19801
U.S.A.
(302) 571-2900

DISTRICT OF COLUMBIA
D.C. Office of Human Rights
2000 14th. St. N.W., 3rd. Floor
Washington, DC 20009
U.S.A.
(202) 939-8740

FLORIDA
Human Relations
325 John Knox Road, Suite 240,
Building F
Tallahassee, FL 32399
U.S.A.
(904) 488-7082
(800) 342-8170

INDIANA
Civil Rights Commission
32 E. Washington St., Ste. 900
Indianapolis, IN 46204
U.S.A.
(317) 232-2600

IOWA
Civil Rights Commission
211 E. Maple St., 2nd. Floor
State Office Building
Des Moines, IA 50319
U.S.A.
(515) 281-4121
(800) 457-4416

KANSAS
Commission on Civil Rights
Landon State Office Building
900 S.W. Jackson, 8th. Floor
Suite 851S
Topeka, KS 66612
U.S.A.
(913) 296-3206

KENTUCKY
Commission on Human Rights
701 W. Muhammad Ali Blvd.
P.O. Box 69
Louisville, KY 40201
U.S.A.
(502) 588-4024

MAINE
Human Rights Commission
State House
Station No. 51
Augusta, ME 04333
U.S.A.
(207) 289-2326

MARYLAND
Commission on Human Relations
20 E. Franklin Street
Baltimore, MD 21202
U.S.A.
(301) 333-1700

MASSACHUSETTS
Comm. Against Discrimination
McCormack State Office Bldg.
1 Ashburton Place
Boston, MA 02108
U.S.A.

MICHIGAN
Department of Civil Rights
303 W. Kalamazoo
Lansing, MI 48913
U.S.A.
(517) 334-6079

MINNESOTA
Department of Human Rights
500 Bremer Building
7th. & Robert Street
St. Paul, MN 55101
U.S.A.
(612) 296-5663

NEW HAMPSHIRE
Commission for Human Rights
61 South Spring Street
Concord, NH 03301
U.S.A.
(603) 271-2767

NEW JERSEY
Division on Civil Rights
Dept. of Law and Public Safety
1100 Raymond Blvd.
Newark, NJ 07102
U.S.A.
(201) 648-2700

NEW MEXICO
Human Rights Commission
930 Baca Street
Santa Fe, NM 87501
U.S.A.
(505) 827-6420

NEW YORK
State Division of Human Rights
55 W. 125th. Street
New York, NY 10027
U.S.A.
(212) 870-8400

NORTH CAROLINA
Human Relations Council
121 W. Jones Street
Raleigh, NC 27603
U.S.A.
(919) 733-7996

APPENDIX 231

MISSOURI
Commission on Human Rights
315 Ellis Boulevard
P.O. Box 1129
Jefferson City, MO 65102
U.S.A.
(314) 751-3325

MONTANA
Human Rights Commission
Room C-317 Cogswell Bldg.
Capitol Station, Box 1728
Helena, MT 59624
U.S.A.
(406) 444-2884

NEBRASKA
Neb. Equal Opportunity Comm.
P.O. Box 94934
301 Centennial Mall, South
Lincoln, NE 68509
U.S.A.
(402) 471-2024

NEVADA
Equal Rights Commission
1515 E. Tropicana, Suite 590
Las Vegas, NV 89158
U.S.A.
(702) 386-5304

NORTH DAKOTA
Department of Labor
State Capitol - 5th. Floor
Bismark, ND 58505
U.S.A.
(701) 224-2660

OHIO
Civil Rights Commission
220 Parsons Avenue
Columbus, OH 43215
U.S.A.
(614) 466-2785

OKLAHOMA
Human Rights Commission
Room 480
2101 N. Lincoln Blvd.
Oklahoma City, OK 73105
U.S.A.
(405) 521-2360

OREGON
Bureau of Labor and Industries
Civil Rights Division
State Office Building
1400 S.W. Fifth Ave.
Portland, OR 97201
U.S.A.
(503) 229-5900

PENNSYLVANIA
Human Relations Commission
101 S. Second Street, Ste. 300
P.O. Box 3145
Harrisburg, PA 17105-3145
U.S.A.
(717) 787-4410

VERMONT
Attorney General of Vermont
Civil Rights Division
Pavilion Office Building
109 State Street
Montpelier, VT 05602
U.S.A.
(802) 828-3171

PUERTO RICO
Dept. of Labor and Human Resources
Anti-Discrimination Unit
505 Munoz Rivera Ave.
Hato Rey, PR 00918
(809) 754-5353

VIRGINIA
Dept. of Labor and Industry
P.O. Box 12064
Richmond, VA 23241
U.S.A.
(804) 786-2376

RHODE ISLAND
Commission for Human Rights
10 Abbott Park Place
Providence, RI 02903
U.S.A
(401) 277-2661

VIRGIN ISLANDS
Department of Labor
P.O. Box 3159 53A. 54A & B
Kronprindfens Gode
Charlotte, Amalie
St. Thomas, VI 00801
U.S.A
(809) 776-4700

SOUTH CAROLINA
Human Affairs Commission
2611 Forest Drive
P.O. Drawer 11009
Columbia, SC 29204
U.S.A
(803) 737-6570

WASHINGTON
Washington State Human Rights Commission
402 Evergreen Plaza Building
711 South Capitol Way
Mail Stop FJ-41
Olympia, WA 98504
U.S.A
(206) 753-6770

SOUTH DAKOTA
Division on Human Rights
State Capitol Building
222 E. Capitol, Suite 11
Pierre, SD 57501
U.S.A
(605) 773-3177

TENNESSEE
Human Development Commission
Capitol Blvd. Bldg. Suite 602
226 Capitol Blvd.
Nashville, TN 37219
U.S.A.
(615) 741-2424

TEXAS
Commission on Human Rights
P.O. Box 13493
Capitol Station
Austin, TX 78711
U.S.A.
(512) 475-1178

UTAH
Industrial Commission
Anti-Discrimination Division
160 E. 3rd. Street, South
P.O. Box 510910
Salt Lake City, UT 84151
U.S.A.
(801) 530-6801

WEST VIRGINIA
Human Rights Commission
1036 Quarrier Street
215 Professional Building
Charleston, WV 25301
U.S.A
(304) 348-2616

WISCONSIN
Department of Industry, Labor
and Human Relations
Equal Rights Division
201 E. Washington Ave.
Madison, WI 53702
U.S.A.
(608) 266-6860

WYOMING
Fair Employment Commission
Hathaway Building
Cheyenne, WY 82002
U.S.A.
(307) 777-7261

Books

How To Hire The Right Person
Denis L. Cauvier, 1993
HRD Press
Amherst, MA
1-800-822-2810
U.S.A.

Games Trainers Play
Edward E. Scannell, 1980
McGraw-Hill
1221 Avenue of the Americas
New York, NY 10020
U.S.A.

Labor and Employment Law Desk Book
Gordon Jackson, 1986
Prentice-Hall, Inc.
Englewood Cliffs, NJ
U.S.A.

Immigration Employment Compliance Handbook
A.T. Fragomen and S.C. Bell, 1987
Clark Boardman Company,
435 Hudson Street
New York, NY 10014
U.S.A.

Modern Personnel Forms
Deborah Launer, Rev. 1988
Warren Gorham & Lamont
210 South Street
Boston, MA 02111
U.S.A.

Current Periodicals

Labor and Employment Law:
Compliance and Litigation
Frederick T. Golder, 1987
Callaghan & Company
3201 Old Glenview Road
Wilmette, IL 60091
U.S.A.

Personnel Administrator
American Society for Personnel
Administration
606 N. Washington Street
Alexandria, VA 22314
U.S.A.
(703) 548-3440

Personnel Journal
P.O. Box 2440
Costa Mesa, CA 92628
U.S.A.
(714) 751-1883

Boardroom Reports
Box 1026
Millburn, NJ 07041
U.S.A.

The Law of the Workplace:
Rights of Employers and Employees
James W. Hunt, 1984
The Bureau of National Affairs, Inc.
1231 25th. Street NW
Washington, DC 20037
U.S.A.

Inc.
38 Commercial Wharf
Boston, MA 02110
U.S.A.
(617) 227-4700

APPENDIX IV

- Employment Law in the 50 States—A Reference for Employers
- Employment History Verifications
- Personnel Forms
- Employment Testing

Employment Law in the 50 States— A Reference for Employers

CUE/NAM
1331 Pennsylvania Ave. NW
Suite 1500-North Lobby
Washington, DC 20004-1703
U.S.A.

Employment Practice Reference Sources
Bureau of National Affairs
1231 25th. Street N.W.
Washington, DC 20037
U.S.A.
(301) 258-1033

Employer's Complete Guide to Immigration
Howard David Deutsch, 1987
Prentice Hall Information Services
Paramus, NJ 07652
U.S.A.

Venture
521 Fifth Ave.
New York, NY 10175-0028
U.S.A.
(212) 682-7373

Bureau of Law and Business
64 Wall Street
Madison, CT 06443
U.S.A.
1-800-553-4569
(203) 245-7448 (CT)

John E. Reid & Associates
233 N. Michigan, Suite 1614
Chicago, IL 60601
U.S.A.
1-800-621-4553
(312) 938-9200

Commerce Clearing House
4025 W. Peterson Ave.
Chicago, IL 60646
U.S.A.
(312) 583-8500

Dartnell, Inc.
4660 Ravenswood Ave.
Chicago, IL 60640
U.S.A.
(312) 561-4000

Stanton Corporation
417 South Dearborn
Chicago, IL 60605
U.S.A.
1-800-621-4553
(312) 922-0970

EEOC
Publications Department
2401 "E" Street, N.W.
Washington, DC 20507
U.S.A.
(202) 634-6922

Employment History Verification

Fidelifacts
50 Broadway
New York, NY 10004
U.S.A.
1-800-223-3140
(212) 425-1520 (NY)

Personnel Forms

Amsterdam Printing & Litho
Wallins Corner Road
Amsterdam, NY 12010
U.S.A.
1-800-833-6231
1-800-342-6116 (NY State)

Equifax Services Inc.
1600 Peachtree Steet, N.W.
Atlanta, GA 30309
U.S.A.
1-800-327-5932

Dartnell, Inc.
4660 Ravenswood Ave.
Chicago, IL 60640
U.S.A.
1-800-621-5463
(312) 561-4000 (IL)

Verified Credentials, Inc.
4010 West 65th. Street
Minneapolis, MN 55435
U.S.A.
(612) 431-1811

Selectform, Inc.
Box 3045
Freeport, NY 11520
U.S.A.
(516) 623-0400

Employee Testing

E.F. Wonderlic & Associates
820 Frontage Road
Northfield, IL 60093
U.S.A.
(312) 446-8900

Consulting Resource Group Ltd. Int.
386-33255 South Fraser Way
Abbotsford, B.C. V2S 2B2
Canada

ETS Test Collection
Educational Testing Service
Princeton, NJ 08541
U.S.A.
(609) 921-9000

London House, Inc.
1550 Northwest Highway
Park Ridge, IL 60028
U.S.A.
1-800-323-5923
(312) 298-7311 (IL)

APPENDIX V

- **Associations for Speakers**
- **Associations for Consultants**
- **Seminar & Workshop Companies**
- **Audio & Video Cassette Sales**
- **Partial List of Topics Offered by Members of the National Speakers Association**

Associations For Speakers

American Society For Training and Development (ASTD)
P.O. Box 5307
Madison, WI 53705
U.S.A.

Australian National Speakers Association
Box 221
Paddington, Qld 4064
Australia

International Platform Association
2564 Berkshire Road
Cleveland Heights, OH 44106
U.S.A.

National Speakers Association (NSA)
1500 South Priest Drive
Tempe, AZ 85281
U.S.A.

Professional Speakers Association
3540 Wilshire Blvd., Suite 310
Los Angeles, CA 90010
U.S.A.

Toastmasters International
2200 N. Grand Ave.
Santa Anna, CA 92711
U.S.A.

Associations For Consultants

American Association of Professional Consultants
9140 Ward Parkway
Kansas City, MO 64114
U.S.A.

American Society of Trial Consultants
Twoson State University
Towson, MD 21204
U.S.A.

Association of Management Consultants
500 N. Michigan Ave.
Chigago, IL 60611
U.S.A.

Association of Management Consulting Firms
230 Park Ave.
New York, NY 10169
U.S.A.

Council of Management Consulting Firms
230 Park Ave.
New York, NY 10169
U.S.A.

Institute of Management Consultants
19 W. 44th St.
New York, NY 10036
U.S.A.

Seminar & Workshop Companies

CAREER TRACKS
1775 38th Street
Boulder, Co.
80301-2639
U.S.A.

KEYE PRODUCTIVITY CENTRE
P.O. Box 3014
Commerce Court Postal Station
Toronto, Ont.
M5L 1K1
Canada

GIBSON INTERNATIONAL SEMINARS
4250 Blenheim Street
Vancouver, B.C.
V6L 2Z4 1-800-663-0336
Canada

WHITEHEAD MORRIS BUSINESS
P.O. Box 1973,
Randburg 2125
South Africa

DENIS L. CAUVIER SEMINARS
74 Boisé des Mûriers
Cantley, Québec
J8V 3L7 (819) 827-5211
Canada

NATIONAL SEMINARS
10 Newgate, Unit #4
Scarborough, Ont.
M1X 1C5
Canada

PADGETT-THOMPSON
P.O. Box 1173,
Commerce Court Postal Station
Toronto, Ont.
M5L 1K1
Canada

DUN AND BRADSTREET EDUCATION SERVICES
P.O. Box 803
Church St. Station
New York, NY 10008
U.S.A.

FRED PRYOR SEMINARS
2000 Johnson Dr.
P.O. Box 8279
Shawnee Mission, KS 66201
U.S.A.

SEMINAR & CONFERENCE MANAGEMENT NETWORK
P.O. Box 582
Edison, NJ 08818-0582
U.S.A.

SEMINARS INTERNATIONAL
15910 Ventura Blvd., Suite 1207
Encino, CA 91436
U.S.A.

Audio & Video Cassette Sales

CAREER TRACK PUBLICATION
1775 38TH Street
Boulder, Co.
8030-2639
U.S.A.

NIGHTINGALE-CONANT CORP
7300 North Lehigh Avenue
Chicago, Ill. 60648
U.S.A.

Partial List of Topics Offered by Members of the National Speakers Association

Advertising/Public Relations
Agriculture
Alcoholism/Drug Abuse
Art, Culture, Music
Athletics/Sports
Business
Careers
Communication
Computers
Consulting
Creativity
Customer Service
Economics
Education
Ethics
Family
Financial & Tax Planning Insurance
Future
Government & Policies
Health & Nutrition
Human Resources/Labour Relations
Humor
Image
Inspirational
International Affairs
Law
Leadership
Management

Marketing/Merchandising
Media
Medical(Dental)
Motivation
Negotiating
Organizational Skills
Patriotic
Performance Improvement
Productivity
Psychology
Real Estate
Relationships
Religion
Retirement
Safety
Sales
Science/Engineering
Speakers Bureau/Service Orgs.
Spouse Programs
Strategic Planning
Stress
Success
Technology
Time/Self Management
Training
Women in Society
Writing